YLAWNDA PEEBL

H.O.P.E.

A JOURNEY THROUGH 150 GLORIOUS DAYS TO FREEDOM

YP GRATITUDE *Journey*

Hold On Pain Ends

Published by Godzchild Publications
a division of Godzchild, Inc.
22 Halleck St., Newark, NJ 07104
www.godzchildproductions.net

Printed in the United States of America 2020 - 1st Edition

Library of Congress Cataloging-in-Publications Data
Hold On Pain Ends/Ylawnda Peebles, D.D., D.H.L

ISBN-13 978-1-942705-62-8
1. Ylawnda Peebles 2. D.D., D.H.L.

GRATITUDE Journey

TABLE OF CONTENTS

30. SHACKLES REMOVED, NOW I EMBRACE MY FREEDOM

31. CHIN UP, SHOULDERS BACK, THOUGHTS TOGETHER

32. WEIGHTS DOWN, CREATIVE CAPITAL INCREASING

33. I HAVE NO ROOM TO FEAR

34. PARADISE IS MY CHOICE

35. I AM PROTECTING MY PARADISE

36. I WILL SHARE MY PARADISE EXPERIENCE

37. MY PARADISE IS GROWING

38. I AM GOING TO LIVE LIFE TO ITS FULLEST

39. I WILL NEVER STOP CREATING MY PARADISE

40. I WILL NEVER FORFEIT MY PARADISE

41. I WILL ALWAYS MAKE LOVE MY HABIT

42. I WILL PRACTICE EMOTIONAL INTELLIGENCE DAILY

43. I CHOOSE TO BRING PEACE TO ALL MY RELATIONSHIPS

44. I REALIZE MY THOUGHTS ARE MY CHOICES

45. I CHOOSE TO SECURE MY FUTURE WITH GRATITUDE

46. I CHOOSE TO LAUGH DAILY

47. I CHOOSE TO LOVE MYSELF

48. LOVE WILL HELP ME CONQUER SOMETHING DIFFICULT

49. I WILL BE GUIDED BY MY SOFTER SIDE

50. MY LOVE SHALL GOVERN MY TIME

51. LOVE SHALL GUIDE MY EVERY STEP

52. I WILL ALWAYS LET LOVE PRECEDE ME

53. WHAT ARE MY SIGNS OF LOVE?

54. I AM CHOOSING LOVE FOR MYSELF AND EVERYONE AROUND ME

55. THE DEVIL IS A LIAR AND GOD IS A PROMISE-KEEPER

56. I AM LEARNING TO BE CONTENT IN MY OWN SKIN

57. I AM CONTENT WITH WAITING

58. I AM CONTENT WITH A DAY WELL LIVED

59. I SEE MY OWN VALUE AND WORTH

60. I SEE MYSELF ENJOYING LIFE TO THE FULLEST

61. I SEE MYSELF ENJOYING PEACE

62. I UNDERSTAND THE NEED FOR JUST 1 MINUTE

63. I AM THE BEST THING THAT GOD EVER CREATED

64. I AM A TRUE SOLDIER IN GOD'S ARMY

65. I AM SOMEBODY

66 I WILL DAILY PROCLAIM WHO I AM

67. I AM GOD'S ANOINTED GIFT

68. I AM WORTHY OF EVERYTHING GOD HAS FOR ME

69. I KNOW MY GOD IS ABLE

70. I WILL CHOOSE LOVE UNTIL IT BECOMES WHO I AM

71. I WILL REMEMBER TO SEIZE THE MOMENT

72. LOVE IS MY FIRST RESPONSE

73. PATIENCE IS MY FIRST RESPONSE

74. I AM WOMAN, HEAR ME ROAR

75. I AM AN EXAMPLE TO MY CHILDREN

76. I AM AN EXAMPLE TO OTHERS

77. I AM OUT OF THE BOX

78. SIMPLY, THANK YOU LORD

79. I AM GOING TO STAND UP AND DO SOMETHING

80. I SHALL RISE UP

81. GOD ALWAYS HAS THE FINAL SAY

82. GOD IS USING ME FOR SOMETHING EXTRAORDINARY

83. I LOVE ME SOME ME

84. I LIKE WHAT I SEE WHEN I AM LOOKING AT ME

85. I WILL LOVE REGARDLESS

86. FORGIVENESS IS THE GREATEST PART OF SELF-LOVE

87. OBSTACLES ARE MY DISGUISED STEPPING STONES

88. STICK-TO-ITIVENESS IS MY GIFT TO ME

89. I WILL STAY THE COURSE

90. TODAY, I CELEBRATE ME

91. I AM CHALLENGING MYSELF TO LET GO

92. I GIVE MYSELF PERMISSION TO LIVE

93. I GIVE MYSELF PERMISSION TO FORGIVE

94. HOW BAD DO I WANT WHAT GOD HAS FOR ME?

95. I WON'T TALK ABOUT IT, I WILL BE ABOUT IT

96. I AM ROYALTY

97. I AM OPENING MY SELF-INFLICTED PRISON BARS

98. I LIKE WHO I AM BECOMING ON THIS JOURNEY

99. WHAT IS MY FAITH CALLING INTO EXISTENCE?

100. PUT A PRAISE ON IT AND GET WHAT YOU DESIRE

101. I AM A QUEEN OF THE KINGDOM

102. BREATHE AND BE

103. I AM DETERMINED TO LIVE MY LIFE

104. MY PRISON DOORS ARE OPEN

105. WHAT AM I DREAMING ABOUT?

106. WHAT AM I DOING WITH MY TIME?

107. I AM A CHILD OF GOD, A BRANCH OF THE TRUE VINE

108. MY NEXT LEVEL REQUIRES HOLINESS

109. TODAY IS THE BEGINNING OF EVERYTHING I EVER WANTED

110. WHO AM I AND WHAT DO I WANT IN MY LIFE?

111. I AM A WOMAN OF TRANSFORMATION

112. I WILL NEVER GET IN MY OWN WAY

113. NOTHING WILL PREVENT ME FROM FLYING HIGH

114. I WILL ASK GOD FOR WHAT I WANT/DESIRE

115. I MUST CREATE A QUIET SPACE IN MY LIFE

116. I WILL TREASURE THE QUIET SPACE CREATED IN MY LIFE

117. IF I KEEP THE FAITH, IT WILL ALWAYS WORK FOR ME

118. NO MORE EXCUSES, I AM RUNNING WITH MY VISION

119. I AM NOT A REPEAT OFFENDER

120. I NOW DANCE IN THE RAIN WITH PURPOSE

121. I NOW SING WITH A PURPOSE

122. I CELEBRATE LOVING ME

123. I AM BOLD, I AM CONFIDENT, I AM FREE

124. I HAVE MY WINGS, NOW IT'S TIME TO FLY

125. I AM IN TOUCH WITH MY FEELINGS

126. PHYSICIAN, HEAL THYSELF

127. MY ABC'S ~ ADMIT IT, BREATHE, GET COUNSEL

128. I HAVE POWER, LOVE, AND A SOUND MIND

129. I AM GOING TO BE ABOUT MY WORK

130. I WILL NEVER DO THESE THINGS AGAIN

131. MY INTEGRITY MUST BE CONSISTENT

132. I WILL INSPIRE OTHERS TO WALK IN INTEGRITY

133. MY INTEGRITY WILL PROTECT MY DESTINY

134. I AM TAKING MY RED CARPET WALK THROUGH SUCCESS

135. I WILL DO WHAT IS RIGHT AND GOD WILL PAY

136. I HAVE THE ABILITY TO CALL THINGS INTO EXISTENCE

137. I WILL HAVE WHAT I SAY

138. I WILL PAY ATTENTION TO WHAT I AM ATTRACTING

139. I WILL NOT DESPISE THE CRAWLING STAGE

140. I AM READY TO LET IT ALL GO

141. MY LIFE MUST BE INTENTIONAL

142. I AM ON THE WISE TRACK TOWARD ACCOMPLISHING MY GOALS

143. I WILL FOCUS ON LIVING AND NOT DYING

144. GOD WILL ALWAYS INTERVENE ON MY BEHALF

145. I HAVE TO BE MORE FOCUSED THAN EVER

146. I WILL BE THE CHANGE I WANT TO SEE IN THE WORLD

147. MY INTEGRITY WILL ALWAYS GO BEFORE ME

148. I WILL WELCOME JESUS INTO MY LIFE

149. AND IT CAME TO PASS

150. I AM HEADED TO MY PRAYER ROOM

1. EXPLOSIVE MANIFESTATIONS

Today, I will express gratitude for everything that life brings my way. I am convinced and compelled to believe that, indeed, all things work together for my good. Therefore, I will look for explosive manifestations of love, grace, and joy. When life throws me unexpected situations, I will continue to search for explosive manifestations. I am grateful for insight, perspective and an opportunity to experience life with those I love.

Today I am grateful for:

Introspective/Reflection Questions:

1. Identify one explosive manifestation that you hope to see materialize in your life within the next 30 days.
2. Reflect on a previous time when an unexpected moment of joy changed your perspective.

GRATITUDE Journey

Homework:

Today, be intentional about smiling more than you usually do. If you desire more love, set an intention to be more loveable. If you desire more joy, be intentional about the joy you bring in every room. Jot down anything unique that may happen today.

2. DON'T DOUBT THE PROMISES OF GOD

Today, I will not give doubt permission to pervade my thoughts, actions, or feelings. I will stand in the promises of God. I am grateful for the Word of God, that reminds me that I am the head and not the tail; above and not beneath; the lender and not the borrower. And I will not allow obstacles, circumstances or distractions to distort or derail my focus. God is not a man that He should lie; nor the son of man that he should repent. Whatever he says, it will manifest. Whatever he promises, He keeps his word. I will rest in that truth, and I will find gratitude in God's promises.

Today I am grateful for:

Introspective/Reflection Questions:

1. When is the last time you struggled with doubt? Why?
2. What did that experience teach you? What can you do, this time, to counteract doubt when it shows up?

Homework:

Find three promises that God made us in the Bible, and write them down on a sticky note, record them on your phone, or post them on social media. Return to these promises whenever doubt tries to invade your space.

3. NEVER GIVE UP

Today, I will be grateful for new opportunities to win. I will be grateful for new doors that are opening. I will also dismiss every thought that tries to disrupt my moment. I believe the saying is true—winners never quit, and quitters never win. With that in mind I will keep my eye on the prize and I will not give up. I may need to take "rest stops" along the way, but giving up is not an option. God has empowered me and equipped me to finish and I will complete everything I set my mind to do, for His glory.

Today I am grateful for:

Introspective/Reflection Questions:

1. Write down a time when you gave up and did not complete a certain goal. What caused you to give up?
2. Now write down a time when you persevered through the difficult obstacle, and you met the goal. What did you do differently?

GRATITUDE *Journey*

Homework:

Identify one short-term goal that you wish to accomplish over the next 7 days. Write it down, and share it with an accountability partner. Then return to this assignment in 7 days to check off that you completed it! Remember: celebrate small victories and be grateful for it all!

4. I AM GETTING OUT OF GOD'S WAY

Today, I will appreciate God for being smarter than me. God is a God who orders steps. God is a God who has great plans for me. God is a God who knows my end from the beginning, and for this reason, I will get out of God's way and let God do what He needs to do in my life. I will express gratitude to every person who points me in the direction of God, and I will pay it forward and help point others in the direction of God as well. I am overwhelmed with joy and anticipation as I prepare for the great things God has in store for me.

Today I am grateful for:

Introspective/Reflection Questions:

1. Name a time when someone you love (sibling, parent, spouse, or friend) went ahead of God and got in His way?
How did you know they were moving in the opposite direction?
2. What did that experience teach you about yourself?

GRATITUDE Journey

Homework:

This week, find a song that you will listen to, whenever you find yourself acting impulsively or impatiently. That song might be a slow calming tune that helps you to meditate or pray. Or, that song might be a fast-paced beat that inspires you to exercise in the gym! Whatever that song is, make it your "Getting out of God's way" song!

5. SOW A GOOD SEED

Today, I am grateful for the principle of sowing and reaping. I truly believe that we reap what we sow. Therefore, I will sow kindness to a stranger, empathy to a loved one, and compassion to a friend. I believe that God honors a kind word, a listening ear, and a loving embrace when we sow with pure intentions and honorable motivations. I am grateful for those who sowed good seed into my life. I am grateful for mentors, mothers, and strangers who were selfless in their abundant compassion for me. I will never forget those who have helped me to become who I am today.

Today I am grateful for:

_____

_____

_____

_____

_____

_____

Introspective/Reflection Questions:

1. When is the last time you sowed a seed (of love, joy, or a generous monetary gift) and experienced a beautiful harvest in return? Reflect on that experience below.
2. Name three people who were selfless enough to pour into you, mentor you, or teach you something you didn't know. List them here and say a short prayer for them before you end your quiet time.

_____

_____

_____

_____

_____

_____

_____

Homework:

If you identified three people in the previous section, take 5 minutes to write a hand-written letter to each individual. Thank them for what they've sown into you. Remind them of how they blessed you. If time permits, mail the letter to their home or hand deliver it to their office. They will forever remember the time you designated to say thank you.

6. I HAVE TO BE IN THE RIGHT PLACE, AT THE RIGHT TIME

I am grateful for divine encounters and miraculous moments. I am grateful that God places people in the right place at the right time, to confirm his will and his word. I am right where I need to be, and I am trusting that when it's time for me to move, God will speak. I am grateful for sensitivity to God's voice and I am looking for God to blow my mind today! Timing is everything and b anticipating a monumental blessing of God's presence and promise.

Today I am grateful for:

Introspective/Reflection Questions:

1. Recall a time where God aligned the right person with the right place at the right time. Write their name and the occasion below.
2. What are you believing God for right now, and do you believe your time table matches God's time table. Why or why not?

GRATITUDE *Journey*

Homework:

The Bible says we have not because we ask not. So put your requests below. Ask God for whatsoever you desire, and also ask God to meet your need(s) by a certain time. Then pay close attention and watch God's miraculous hand work in your life.

7. I WILL WALK BY FAITH

Today, I will not trust what my eyes are telling me, and what my feelings want me to believe. Where there is fear, I will have faith. Where this is doubt, I will have trust. Where there are questions, I will turn to God for my answer. He is the God of all resolution and completion. I am grateful that the Word gives us biblical characters to compare our lives to, and in this moment, I will recall the disciple, and later apostle, Peter; who walked on the water of faith and pursued after Christ in the midst of turbulent winds and tumultuous storms. I trust that if God did it for Peter, then God can do it for me!

Today I am grateful for:

Introspective/Reflection Questions:

1. Who inspires you, in the Old Testament, to keep the faith?
2. Who inspires you, in the New Testament, to keep the faith?

GRATITUDE Journey

Homework:

Create a "forget it" chart, and list all of the things you hope to forget that tried to discourage you, demean you, and disparage you. For example, "I choose to forget the negative words they said, the classes I could not pass, the job I did not receive." As you list each area, remember to say "Thank you." God's plans for you are greater than what you may have lost.

8. I WILL LET THE MIND OF CHRIST BE IN ME

I am grateful today for my mind. I am grateful for logic, recall, and a healthy memory. I am grateful for the things I can remember, and I'm even grateful for the things God allowed me to forget. As strong as my mind is, I am aware that my mental capacity is not stronger than the mind of Christ. Therefore, I will let the mind of Christ be in me. I will allow Christ to reign, rule, and regulate my thoughts, my imagination, my emotions, and my choices. I believe that God knows better than me, and His thoughts toward me are greater than I can ever imagine. So Lord, here's my mind...take it, and in exchange, I will joyfully accept the mind of Christ.

Today I am grateful for:

Introspective/Reflection Questions:

1. Finish this sentence: the greatest memory I had this week is:
2. Identify something that was difficult to forget, but over time, God helped you to let it go.

GRATITUDE *Journey*

Homework:

Create a "forget it" chart, and list all of the things you hope to forget that tried to discourage you, demean you, and disparage you. For example, "I choose to forget the negative words they said, the classes I could not pass, the job I did not receive." As you list each area, remember to say "Thank you." God's plans for you are greater than what you may have lost.

9. GOD HAS THE FINAL SAY

Today, I give thanks for all things, including the process toward the promise. I will not allow myself to become discouraged by the "middle seasons." In other words, I will not let the wilderness convince me that God is finished. Instead, I will stand on this undeniable truth: God has the final say. God has the final say about my health, my wealth, my relationships, and my future. God is the ultimate Judge and until His verdict is given, I will rest in the promises of God. I am so glad that I am not in control of my life, and that the opinion of others, does not dictate my destiny. God is the author and finisher of my faith, and I will rejoice in the conclusion that he has already decided about me.

Today I am grateful for:

Introspective/Reflection Questions:

1. What is the most challenging thing about this "middle season?"
2. What is the greatest lesson you've learned during this "middle season?"

GRATITUDE *Journey*

Homework:

Write a "thank you" letter to God as if what you've been praying for, and believing for, has already happened.

10. I WILL TRUST WHAT I CAN'T SEE

Today, I will show gratitude for everything I can see—my family, my friends, my reflection, my blessings. I will give myself to nature and appreciate the fresh air, the green trees, the small insects, and the beautiful butterflies. I will also remind myself that there is another world beyond what my eyes can see, that God is keenly aware of, and responsible for. I have no doubt that God is in control, and the more I give thanks for what I can see, the more I will trust Him for what I can't see. Even though I do not know how the situation will turn out, I will trust that all things will work together for my good; so if it's not good yet...then God's not done working yet!

Today I am grateful for:

Introspective/Reflection Questions:

1. Pay attention to the first five things that happened to you this morning. Give thanks for each.
2. Who has been a consistent example, in your life, on the importance of trusting God?

GRATITUDE *Journey*

Homework:

Write down your favorite scripture verse about "trust" and commit it to memory this week.

11. I WILL GET THE DESIRES OF MY HEART

Today I will choose gratitude instead of complaint. I will choose peace instead of confusion. I will intentionally remove anything that is blocking my clarity. I will vacuum out negative thoughts, negative words, and negative opinions. I am certain that God will give me the desires of my heart, and I am committed to enjoying the abundance of life and living on earth, as it is in heaven.

Today I am grateful for:

Introspective/Reflection Questions:

1. What are two distractions that need to be removed from your life?
2. How will you keep your heart clear from the distractions you just listed?

GRATITUDE Journey

Homework:

Come up with a plan to "remain clear" and focused over the next five days. What can be eliminated from your normal routine to keep the static out?

12. TRUST GOD'S PROCESS

Today, I am grateful for every step. Like a little baby who learns how to walk for the first time, the process may seem arduous in the beginning—but over time, she gains strength for the journey. One day, she crawls. Another day she tumbles. But finally, she walks successfully across the living room floor, and her parents rejoice triumphantly for her safe arrival. I will remember this when I think of God's process for my life. I will trust Him even when I fall. I will trust him even if I fail. I will trust that He will be standing by my side, and cheering me on as I make it to my destination successfully. Winning is the only option for me!

Today I am grateful for:

Introspective/Reflection Questions:

1. What are the advantages of failure? How might failure and falling help you to trust God more?

2. In life, the question is not if you will have problems, but how you are going to deal with your problems. If the ossibility of failure were erased, what would you attempt to achieve?

Homework:

Share this quote with someone today. The essence of man is imperfection. Know that you're going to make mistakes. The fellow who never makes a mistake takes his orders from one who does. Wake up and realize this: Failure is simply a price we pay to achieve success.

13. I AM A MOUNTAIN MOVER

Today, I am grateful for obstacles. I am grateful that obstacles are opportunities for new levels of faith. I am a mountain mover. Whatever I determine to do, I will accomplish. Whatever I set my mind on to attain, I will achieve. There is nothing too hard for God, and nothing that I cannot do with his strength. I will speak to the mountain until it moves. I will climb the mountain until I arrive. I will overthrow the mountains until my thoughts transform into results. This is going to be an award-winning season in my life, and every mountain must move!

Today I am grateful for:

Introspective/Reflection Questions:

1. Name a personal mountain that you will work to remove
2. Name a professional mountain that you are actively working on as well.

GRATITUDE Journey

Homework:

When these mountains are removed, who will you help? Remember we are blessed to be a blessing, so write a short vision statement for those you desire to assist.

14. I AM GOING TO BUILD MY SPIRITUAL AND EMOTIONAL CAPITAL

Today, I will express gratitude for small victories. Indeed, Rome wasn't built in a day so I will not force myself to rush this moment. Instead, I will enjoy the marathon. Every day, I will invest in my spiritual and emotional wellbeing. Each day, I will take a little time to enjoy the view. I will not allow the busyness of the world to contaminate the fluidity of my focus. I will intentionally build equity spiritually, emotionally, and relationally, and everyone who encounters me today, will be better because of it.

Today I am grateful for:

Introspective/Reflection Questions:

1. Celebrate one small "health" victory that you have achieved over the last 30 days.
2. Identify one small "financial" victory that you have accomplished over the last 30 days.

GRATITUDE *Journey*

Homework:

Consider your spiritual, emotional, and relational victories, and write down one realistic goal that you can accomplish over the next 24 hours. For some it may be to extend your time of prayer. For another, it could be to call a loved one and check on them for 15 minutes. Write your victories below and then execute with gratitude!

15. I WON'T TURN BACK

I am grateful for every detour and every set-back because now I know that they all prepared me for a comeback. But I am determined not to turn back. I will not look to the left or the right. I will not compare my pace with someone else. I believe that everything for me is for me, and I am grateful for the good days, the bad days, and every day in between. This is not a time to cry about what I lost. This is a time to rejoice about what I have left!

Today I am grateful for:

Introspective/Reflection Questions:

1. What was one financial setback you experienced this year? What did it teach you?
2. Identify one physical setback as well. How did that temporary setback make you feel?

GRATITUDE Journey

Homework:

Write a rebound statement for each financial, physical, and relational setback. The statement should state what your new goal is, and what you learned from that setback. For example: Financially, I didn't expect to need a new car this year, but I will double my savings by the end of this year.

16. THANK YOU GOD FOR MY BRAIN TRANSPLANT

I choose gratitude today for the big things and the small things. For a change in mindset, and for the discipline to follow-through. Everything about me will change because of the way I think. Before, I would allow negative thoughts to seep into my being. Now, I have allowed God to change my mind. I have submitted my desires to His, and He has given me a complete brain transplant. I see bigger for myself than I did before. I see brighter for my family than I did before. And I am healthier now—emotionally, relationally, financially, and spiritually-than I have ever been!

Today I am grateful for:

Introspective/Reflection Questions:

1. How will you protect yourself from negative thoughts?
2. What is one dream that you want to make true for someone else?

GRATITUDE Journey

Homework:

Create a chart and list 5 old ways you used to think on the left hand side. Then create 5 new ways of thinking on the right hand side. Compare and contrast and share with your friends so they can keep you accountable.

17. I SHALL EMBRACE THE POSITIVE ME

Why sorrow in the deficits when I can rejoice about the benefits? Why sulk about my weaknesses when I can smile about my strengths? I am resilient. I bounce back quickly. Nothing can keep me down even if it takes me down. I am alive. I am breathing. I add value to every room I enter. I am the gift that keeps on giving. I am not my past, and I will not stay stuck in my present. Instead, I will embrace the positive me; the glowing me; the growing me, and I will say "thank you" for every age and stage that God has blessed me to see.

Today I am grateful for:

Introspective/Reflection Questions:

1. What positive thing do you bring to the table consistently?
2. When is the last time you caught yourself glowing? What were you wearing? Where were you going?

GRATITUDE Journey

Homework:

Think about small ways you can grow and glow daily, and then set an intention to grow and glow on a daily basis. Today, your grow goal may be to learn a new vocabulary word. Or, it may be to walk/run an extra mile in the morning. Your glow goal may be to smile more and to hug tighter. Design your grow/glow goals and post them somewhere you can see them often.

18. I CAN CALL ANYTHING INTO EXISTENCE

Because I trust in the Lord with all of my heart, I trust that He leads me and guides me to the right places that I need to go. He is the God of the open door, and the God of the closed door. Therefore, I will be grateful for the words he has given me, for life is locked inside of every word I say. Today, I will guard my words and protect my destiny because I know the power that works within me. I can call anything into existence, so today, I call healing, hope, restoration, reconciliation, opportunities, promotions, love, and joy.

Today I am grateful for:

Introspective/Reflection Questions:

1. Name a time when God opened a door that you know, for a fact, happened because of God.
2. Recall a moment when God closed a door that needed to be closed in order for you to become who you are today.

Homework:

What are 3 things you really want emotionally, physically, relationally, or financially? Write them down and call them into existence for the next 7 days. Repeat them often. Share them with people trust. Then look for the manifestation of what you said.

19. AND IT CAME TO PASS

I am grateful for the word of God that gives life-changing principles in edible arrangements. I believe every open door will swing wide open for me. I believe every seed I sow will bring bountiful blessings my way. And I believe that love sets the tone for life filled with blessings. For this I am grateful. I am grateful for doors, seed, and love. Nothing will stop me from getting everything God has for me. It shall come to pass!

Today I am grateful for:

Introspective/Reflection Questions:

1. What do you want to come to pass by the end of the day?
2. What do you want to come to pass by the end of the year?

GRATITUDE *Journey*

Homework:

Think on where you want to be, and what you need to become that. If it's happier, what do you need? If it's stronger, what do you need? If it's richer or more balanced, what do you need? Everything begins with a positive thought and the determination to make it happen.

20. I AM GETTING OFF THE FERRIS WHEEL

Life is always moving. Opportunities come a dime a dozen, and a mile per minute. Today, I will be grateful for the technological advances in life and the resources and inventions that make life easier, but I will also lean into the simple things of life: clean air, a tall glass of water, laughter; a cool breeze; and fresh fruit. I am getting off the Ferris wheel of competition and comparison. I am getting off the Ferris wheel of rushing through life and not paying attention to the still, small voice of God. I am getting off the Ferris wheel, and deciding to take the stairs. Life is too short to miss it in the rush.

Today I am grateful for:

Introspective/Reflection Questions:

1. What is a simple blessing for which you are grateful?
2. What is the last thing you bought for yourself to simplify your life?

Homework:

Today, drink more water, and breathe more deeply. Create 7 intentional moments to slow down and pay attention to the beauty that is your life. Once you do it, treat yourself to something simple, but something nice.

21. I AM CREATING A NO REGRETS LIFE

Everything that has happened to ME, has happened FOR me. For this, I am grateful. I will not spend one moment wallowing in regret. I will not worry about tomorrow. I will let tomorrow handle itself. This day, I will run into every blessing God has prepared for me. I will thank God for the lessons, the blessings, the great moments and the not-so-good ones too; I shall have no regrets. That is the life I want to create for myself, and that is the only life that is worth living.

Today I am grateful for:

Introspective/Reflection Questions:

1. Name one lesson that this last month has taught you.
2. Name one blessing that came out of a moment of regret.

GRATITUDE Journey

Homework:

Write a thank you letter to your mistakes. Write a thank you letter to your ex. Write a thank you letter to your regrets. And once you finish it, shred it and give God praise for the new wind of blessings that are coming your way.

22. I CAN SEE CLEARLY NOW...THE RAIN IS GONE

The rain is a beautiful creation. It replenishes the earth. It protects us from drought. It allows us to experience the beauty of nature. The rain is a cleanser for the world and a cleanser for the soul. I will choose, today, to be grateful for the rainy seasons of life—for, now that the rain is gone, I can see clearly now. I can see everything as it is, and everyone as they are. I am grateful for the cleanser.

Today I am grateful for:

Introspective/Reflection Questions:

1. In what areas do you need cleansing?
2. How do you re-set your life when it feels too congested?

Homework:

Carve out time for cleansing. For some, that may mean organizing your closets. For others, that may mean visiting your therapist. For another, that may mean getting a manicure/pedicure. But decide what your weekly cleansing moment will look like, and do it.

23. I WILL OBEY GOD'S CALL TO ACTION

Today, I am grateful for the reward that obedience brings. Abraham received one word "Go" and obeyed. As a result, he became the father of many nations and his wife Sarah bore a child. Mary received one visitation and obeyed. As a result, she became the mother of Jesus and carried our Savior in her womb. I am carrying something great, and I am grateful to be called. As a sign of my appreciation, I will obey God's call today, tomorrow, and always.

Today I am grateful for:

Introspective/Reflection Questions:

1. What has God been calling you to do, that you've been ignoring?
2. What obstacle continues to get in the way of your goal?

GRATITUDE Journey

Homework:

Today, eliminate every obstacle and quit hitting the snooze button. Confess that you will not ignore the calling, and pursue it with all of your might.

24. I AM A BLESSING MAGNET

Everything attached to me wins. Everything around me will prosper. I am the head and not the tail. I am above and not beneath. I am the lender and not the borrower. I attract health, wealth, and joy. The favor on my life is contagious and I am grateful that God has blessed me abundantly so that I can bless others immensely. I am a blessing magnet, and everything I touch, will know that God is with me.

Today I am grateful for:

Introspective/Reflection Questions:

1. What is the last big blessing you received?
2. What is the next big blessing you are praying for and believing for?

Homework:

Today, share your last big blessing with a friend. Then, ask how you can pray for their blessing. Pray for them fervently, and remember: what God does for others, He will surely do for you.

25. I AM SO GRATEFUL, I'LL EVEN DANCE IN THE RAIN

There are no sad days, only delayed sunny days. There are no dark days, only moments before the dawning of a new day. The time zone proves that someone can be standing in the same moment and experience a different perspective because of timing. Today, I will wait, in joyful anticipation for the times to change; for the joy to return; and for the rain to end. While I am waiting, I will dance in the rain as if no one is watching. Life is supposed to be fun, and I won't let anything steal my joy!

Today I am grateful for:

Introspective/Reflection Questions:

1. What is your favorite song to dance to?
2. Who is your favorite artist to listen to?

GRATITUDE Journey

Homework:

Take a moment and create a DANCE playlist. Include your favorite artists and your favorite songs. Then, take a moment—at the gym, or in the kitchen—to dance the night away!.

26. I AM STRONG, SO I WILL SURVIVE

I am a winner. I am a survivor. I am not a quitter. I am not mediocre. Today, I choose to be grateful for my strength—the strength I already have and the strength I am developing over time. The same way God told Joshua to be strong and courageous, I am telling everyone around me to do the same. The joy of the Lord is my strength, and when I am strong, I attract survivors. Therefore, I will not quit. I will not stop. I will survive.

Today I am grateful for:

Introspective/Reflection Questions:

1. Recall a time when your strength helped get you through.
2. Who is the strongest person around you? Who is your rock?

Homework:

Take your "strong" friend out to eat and give them a handwritten thank you card. Thank them for being a model of strength, and ask them how you can help strengthen their lives the way they strengthened yours.

27. I AM USHERING IN THE DESIRES OF MY HEART

The same way ushers escort guests to their seats for a show, and the same way worship teams usher worshippers into the presence of the Lord, I am grateful for God being the ultimate Usher of my life. He has empowered me to speak those things that are not as though they were; and every time I do that, I usher in the desire of my heart. Today, I choose to usher in grace, truth, and forgiveness.

Today I am grateful for:

Introspective/Reflection Questions:

1. How can you usher in more grace today?
2. How can you usher in more truth today?

GRATITUDE Journey

Homework:

What is your biggest desire in this moment? Is it peace? Is it joy? It is forgiveness? Is it love? Find a way to usher in whatever you desire, and allow God to take the lead. Don't force it. Allow it.

28. I AM LAYING ASIDE EVERY WEIGHT

Lord, thank you for the weight! And thank you for allowing me to lay down all bad weight. Because I am committed to physical health, I understand the beauty and burden of weight. Some want to lose weight and some want to gain it. But in order to succeed, we have to exercise with "weights" in order to work off our negative weight. Today, I am choosing to be grateful for all of it—for the weight I don't want, and for the weights I need in order to be a better version of me. I am grateful for the ability to let go of every negative weight that is holding me back.

Today I am grateful for:

Introspective/Reflection Questions:

1. Which weights (spiritually) do you want to lay aside?
2. Which weights (physically) do you want to lose or gain?

GRATITUDE *Journey*

Homework:

Some goals can't be achieved without asking for help. Today, hire a fitness trainer or ask a friend to be your accountability partner. Create a 5 day plan to eat right, and work out consistently. Once you accomplish that goal, create a 7 day plan, then a 12 day plan, then a 21 day plan until you are able to sustain your own commitments.

29. I WILL LAY ASIDE ALL UNFORGIVENESS

One of the greatest weights in my life has been unforgiveness. I am grateful that I serve a God who forgives me, and I will pray for the power to forgive others. I now understand that forgiveness is the gift I give myself, so I will actively and intentionally seek forgiveness from those I have wronged, and I will seek to forgive those who have wronged me. My goal is a clear heart and a long life!

Today I am grateful for:

Introspective/Reflection Questions:

1. Is there anyone you have wronged that may be in need of an apology?
2. Is there anyone who has wronged you, that may be in need of forgiveness?

GRATITUDE Journey

Homework:

Keep your heart clear. Call the person you may have ignored for a while. Receive grace and extend forgiveness today, tomorrow, and always.

30. SHACKLES REMOVED, NOW I EMBRACE MY FREEDOM

No more shackles, no more chains, no more bondage I am free. Today, I stand in my freedom. I rejoice in my liberty. I am no longer bound, shaken, derailed, distracted, and overloaded. I am free. I am determined to walk in my freedom today. I am determined to live a life of freedom. I will not allow the opinions of others or the pain from my past to paralyze me from my next victory. I embrace FREEDOM!

Today I am grateful for:

Introspective/Reflection Questions:

1. Name a time when the opinion of others became a shackle.
2. Name a time when the pain from your past paralyzed you.

Homework:

Write a freedom poem today. It can be short. It can be long. It can rhyme. It can be a non-rhyming poem. But take a moment and express your gratitude for newfound freedom in poetic form. Share it on social media once you're done.

31. CHIN UP, SHOULDERS BACK, THOUGHTS TOGETHER

I am determined. I am focused. I am centered. I will not back down. Today, as I prepare for a day of success and achievement, I will enter into every situation with a heart filled with gratitude. I am thankful for focus. I am thankful for discipline. My chin is up, my shoulders are back. My thoughts are together. Winning is the only option today!

Today I am grateful for:

Introspective/Reflection Questions:

1. What helps you to focus?
2. Who distracts you?

GRATITUDE *Journey*

Homework:

Now that you've named your focus assets and your focus liabilities, avoid those who distract you, and connect with those who advance you. Don't compromise!

32. WEIGHTS DOWN, CREATIVE CAPITAL INCREASING

Now that the weights have been removed, I am lighter. I glide through the day with ease and focus. I am grateful that everything is increasing. My joy is increasing. My love is increasing, and my creative capital is increasing. My thoughts are transforming into ideas. My ideas are transforming into plans. My plans are shaping my purpose, and my purpose is helping other people! Thank you for the removal of the weights, let the next level begin!

Today I am grateful for:

Introspective/Reflection Questions:

1. What is your purpose?
2. How is your life moving in the direction of your purpose?

GRATITUDE Journey

Homework:

Today, fast from social media. Every time you want to visit a social media page, use that time to plan for purpose. The goal today is only to do things that will advance your purpose.

33. I HAVE NO ROOM TO FEAR

Fear does not live here. Shame does not rent here. Condemnation does not belong here. Pain must not remain here. There is a no fear zone, and today, I am grateful for the boundaries I set for myself. Instead of fear, I will choose faith. Instead of focusing on those who don't like me, I will cherish the friends and family members who are crazy about me. I am walking into every door with faith and no fear today!

Today I am grateful for:

Introspective/Reflection Questions:

1. Who lights up when you walk into the room?
2. Who do you light up for, when they walk into the room?

GRATITUDE Journey

Homework:

Today, spend some quality time with the "lights of your life." Take them out for lunch. Facetime them if they aren't close. But give them some quality time, and when they ask why tell them "just because you light up my life."

34. PARADISE IS MY CHOICE

Today, I will be grateful for paradise. Some may call it nirvana. Others may call it heaven. For me, it is a place of peace and rest. It is a place of safety and relaxation. It is a place where I am centered. Paradise is my choice, and I will choose it today and every day.

Today I am grateful for:

Introspective/Reflection Questions:

1. Where do you feel most safe? Which room in your house or which place in the world?
2. How do you center yourself? Do you listen to music? Do you meditate?

GRATITUDE *Journey*

Homework:

Now that you've identified your safe space and your centering actions, carve out some time this week to visit that space, and center yourself for about three hours. Unplug from anything that might distract you and then journal about what you discovered.

35. I AM PROTECTING MY PARADISE

I am grateful for the love I feel today. I am grateful for the rest I experienced last night. I am grateful for the beautiful weather, and the place I can rest in the shade, amidst a world filled with noise and chaos. To ensure that I am all that God wants me to be, I will protect my paradise. I will protect myself from negative words, toxic relationships, and unnecessary thoughts. Everything will work out just fine, because my paradise is protected!

Today I am grateful for:

Introspective/Reflection Questions:

1. What does a perfect day look like to you?
2. What does a perfect day feel like to you?

GRATITUDE Journey

Homework:

If life isn't so perfect, how can you craft a life that thrives in the midst of imperfection? Paint a picture. Sing a song. Do something "out of the ordinary" today, and create a paradise in the midst of an imperfect situation.

36. I WILL SHARE MY PARADISE EXPERIENCE

This joy that I have, the world didn't give it to me. This joy that I have, the world can't take it away. God gave me this joy, and like the light of the world, he doesn't want me to hide it under a bushel. So I am committing today to share my paradise with others. I will share love, light, and well wishes with everyone with whom I come into contact today; the stranger, the friend, the family member— the next-door neighbor. Everybody gets a taste of paradise today!

Today I am grateful for:

Introspective/Reflection Questions:

1. How can you share more love today?
2. How can you extend your paradise to a stranger today?

Homework:

Grab an extra $20 from the ATM today. Surprise someone with a gift they didn't see coming. Either pay for their groceries in the supermarket, or buy them a cup of coffee in the Starbucks line. Maybe treat your boss to lunch. But do it as a reminder to share your paradise with others.

37. MY PARADISE IS GROWING

I am beautifying everything around me. I am empowering everyone who meets me. I am blessed to be a blessing, and I am growing to help others grow. I am not selfish. I am not self-absorbed. I will not become a stumbling block for others. Instead, I will be a staircase. When others see me, they will be inspired to go higher. They will be encouraged to keep going, and keep growing. As I grow, I will encourage others to grow. I am grateful for the path that brought me here, and I want nothing more than for the entire world to grow as well!

Today I am grateful for:

Introspective/Reflection Questions:

1. Who do you want to help in a tangible way? Name them here.
2. How can you help them with the resources and relationships that you have?

GRATITUDE Journey

Homework:

Pick up the phone and determine to help one person in a tangible way. Help is not always monetary. Some help is through prayer, a referral, a task completed for them. But ask them how you can help and don't let them hang up until they give you an answer.

38. I AM GOING TO LIVE LIFE TO ITS FULLEST

Nothing will stop me. Nothing will break me. Nothing will discourage me. I am ready for new levels. I am ready for fresh relationships. I am ready to discover new paths to joy, and I am excited about what life will bring today. I will fill my tank today as a reminder to live my life to the fullest. I will charge my phone today, as a reminder to be charged up and ready to receive the fulness that God has in store for me. It's an honor to be alive and my gratitude will be proven by my commitment to make every minute count!

Today I am grateful for:

Introspective/Reflection Questions:

1. When is the last time you filled up someone's tank?
2. When is the last time you took the stairs instead of the elevator? This could also be a metaphor for taking the long route without rushing to get where you are going.

GRATITUDE Journey

Homework:

Before you do anything else today, fill up your tank and remember this is a spiritual practice. When you see your gas tank on full, let it remind you to fulfill your dreams and fill every moment of your day with joy.

39. I WILL NEVER STOP CREATING MY PARADISE

If life is what we make it, then I will design my day intentionally. Who can I inspire? Who can I encourage? Who can I hug tighter? Who can I listen to deeper? I will never stop helping others, and I will never stop loving others. This paradise I have found, is an inner peace, cultivated by God's joy—I will say "thank you" for every mountain and valley, and never stop creating my paradise.

Today I am grateful for:

Introspective/Reflection Questions:

1. Who can you hug today who may not have received love in a long time?
2. Who can you listen to deeper today?

GRATITUDE Journey

Homework:

If you have children, take some time to really step into their world. If you have parents/guardians, take some time to really hear their heart. Let them talk to you about whatever is on their mind. And give them your undivided attention. This will bring so much joy to their lives, even if they don't realize it right now.

40. I WILL NEVER FORFEIT MY PARADISE

Quitters never win, and winners never quit. Therefore, I shall not quit. Even when the winds and waves of life try to mess up the beautiful day that awaits me, I will push all distractions away. I will push all obstacles away. I am God's workmanship. He has made me fearfully and wonderfully; and if He didn't forfeit at the cross, I won't forfeit at this crossroads. I will live to welcome others into this glorious paradise.

Today I am grateful for:

Introspective/Reflection Questions:

1. Name a time when you wanted to quit.
2. Name a time when you persevered despite the odds.

Homework:

Listen to "Don't Quit" by Smokie Norful today. Let it be a consistent reminder of God's purpose and plan for your life.

41. I WILL ALWAYS MAKE LOVE MY HABIT

God's love is contagious. God's love is infectious. Because I am a child of God, I will love like God. I will love the loveable. I will love the unlovable. I will love those I enjoy being around, and I will love those whose presence requires a little more prayer. Nevertheless, I will make love my habit. It is reaction. It is my reflex. It is the starting point, and the finish line. I am grateful for the people who genuinely love me, and I am grateful for the opportunity to love others radically today.

Today I am grateful for:

Introspective/Reflection Questions:

1. When I say "love the loveable" who is the first person that comes to mind? Write their initials below.
2. When I say "love the unlovable" who is the first person that comes to mind? Write their initials below.

GRATITUDE *Journey*

Homework:

Take 60 seconds to pray for the loveable person you mentioned above. Take 120 seconds to pray for the unlovable person you mentioned above. Then pray for your heart that it never stops loving, no matter what happens to it.

42. I WILL PRACTICE EMOTIONAL INTELLIGENCE DAILY

I am in control of my emotions. I am in control of my expressions. I am not thrown off by others' opinions of me, and I am not going to take others' criticism of me personally. I will be everything God has designed me to be, personally and professionally. Every room I enter into today, I will practice emotional intelligence. I am grateful for this daily exercise of speaking life into dark places, and speaking strength into weak moments. This is just a moment, but it will not last forever.

Today I am grateful for:

Introspective/Reflection Questions:

1. Recall a time when someone said something that hurt your feelings.
2. Recall a time when someone's encouragement really brightened your day.

GRATITUDE Journey

Homework:

Aim to be the one who brightens days, not the one who hurts feelings. Say kind words. Look people in their eye. Try not to text and talk. Give people your undivided attention, to the best of your ability. When you leave their presence, give them a good, warm hug.

43. I CHOOSE TO BRING PEACE TO ALL MY RELATIONSHIPS

Because I am a carrier of peace, and because I am a dispenser of peace, peace is the consequence of every conversation I have. Peace is the end result of every meeting, every decision, and every difficult situation. Today, I am thankful for the peace that comes independent of possessions, position, or a platform. This peace comes directly from knowing God and being known by God. How amazing is this wonderful peace!

Today I am grateful for:

Introspective/Reflection Questions:

1. What does peace mean to you?
2. How do you maintain your peace in the midst of a noisy world?

GRATITUDE Journey

Homework:

Find some peaceful music and play it on your way to work, or as you are commuting to church. Let peace serenade your home, your car, and your relationships today.

44. I REALIZE MY THOUGHTS ARE MY CHOICES

No one is responsible for my thoughts but me. No one can push me over the edge but me. My joy is my responsibility. My gratitude is my responsibility. Therefore, I will invest into good thoughts, and only make wise choices. I will be quick to hear and slow to speak, and when I am stressed, I will pause and get some ice cream, or a pedicure, or a massage or take a beautiful walk around my neighborhood. Whatever I must do to keep my life infused with positive thoughts, I will do so.

Today I am grateful for:

Introspective/Reflection Questions:

1. Talk about the last "unwise choice" you made. What did it teach you?
2. Now recall the last "wise choice" you made. How did it help you?

GRATITUDE *Journey*

Homework:

Make a short list of the crucial decisions you need to make, and/or major bills you may need to pay. Then ask yourself "is this wise? Is this realistic? Is there a simpler way to achieve this goal." Share it with someone you trust, and remember to walk in wisdom.

45. I CHOOSE TO SECURE MY FUTURE WITH GRATITUDE

We only have one life, and this day is not a rehearsal. This is the best day of my life, and I am grateful for another 24 hours to live purposefully. Today, I choose to secure my future with gentle, kind, and loving thoughts of gratitude. I will start with simple things to be grateful for, and then finish with the "big things" for which I am grateful. My gratitude is my attitude, and my attitude determines my altitude!

Today I am grateful for:

Introspective/Reflection Questions:

1. What are some simple things for which you are grateful?
2. What are some "big things" for which you are grateful?

GRATITUDE Journey

Homework:

Today listen to "Grateful" by Hezekiah Walker, and think on the list you created above.

46. I CHOOSE TO LAUGH DAILY

Laughter is great medicine. It heals relationships. It helps during difficult moments. It reconnects people who have had a disagreement. It is a balm that brings healing to the soul. Today, I will laugh on purpose. I will laugh with myself. I will laugh at myself, and I will laugh with others. I will look for clean fun and harm less environments where joy and laughterare fostered, and I will lean into all of it, and take a breath. LOL!

Today I am grateful for:

Introspective/Reflection Questions:

1. What is the most embarrassing thing you've ever done?
2. Who do you laugh the most with?

Homework:

Find a comedy show that you enjoy on Netflix or Youtube, and treat yourself to a good laugh. Or, if you have a favourite funny movie, pop some popcorn, change into your pajamas and laugh the night away!

47. I CHOOSE TO LOVE MYSELF

I cannot love from an empty cup. I cannot pour into others without pouring into myself. So while I am grateful forthe moments to speak life into others, today, I choose to speak life into myself. I am healed. I am whole. I am healthy. I am capable. I am beautiful. I am more than a conqueror, and I look good! Today, I will love myself the way Jesus told us to love ourselves. He commanded us to love our neighbors as ourselves, as a reminder to love us before we try to love others. This is my central commitment today!

Today I am grateful for:

Introspective/Reflection Questions:

1. What do you love about yourself?
2. What do you love about your life?

GRATITUDE Journey

Homework:

Create an "I like me/I love me" journal, and each day for the next 21 days, identify something "great" about you that causes you to love yourself more. For example: I like the way I smile. I like the way I encourage others. I love the way I approach life's challenges. Find 21 ways to love yourself today, and spread that love with the world!

48. LOVE WILL HELP ME CONQUER SOMETHING DIFFICULT

Difficult days come. Loved ones pass away. Family members become ill. Downsizing happens. Financial ups and downs are to be expected. But love will help me conquer anything. Today, I choose the things that matter—not the material wealth, but the relational wealth. Today I choose to invest in people and not projects. I choose to spend time thinking about how I will make a difference in the world by serving those who are not as fortunate as me. Love wll conquer anything, and I am grateful for the unbreakable bond, blessing, and gift of love.

Today I am grateful for:

Introspective/Reflection Questions:

1. Who has made your life better?
2. Who has encouraged you in ways that lifted you up?

Homework:

Today, focus on people not projects. Focus on people not promotion. Focus on poeple not prizes. Why? Because people are God's greatest gifts to us. Focus on the people who makes you smile, who give you hope, who have changed your life - and do something tangible to show your appreciation for two people in particular.

49. I WILL BE GUIDED BY MY SOFTER SIDE

God created me this way. There is nothing wrong with me. I am strong and sensitive, I am courageous and curious. I am versatile and vulnerable. I am fiercely me, and also evolving into a great version of myself. Today, I will embrace every part of who I am— including the softer sides of me. I will not be defensive or aggressive. Instead, I will appreciate my unique perspective and I will allow the door to open for me. This is the beauty of being me—God is excited about opening doors that I don't need to touch!

Today I am grateful for:

Introspective/Reflection Questions:

1. What's a "weird" thing about you that you love?
2. What "girly" things do you do that make you, YOU?

GRATITUDE Journey

Homework:

Today allow the door to be opened for you. Ask for help. Smie and say thank you. Try not to touch one door today, and see what that has taught you about you own life.

50. MY LOVE SHALL GOVERN MY TIME

I once heard it said that if you don't tell your time where to go, your time will tell you! I love and am grateful for the 24 hours we get in every new day. I am grateful for every minute and every second. And for this reason, I will cover, protect, guard, and govern my time. My rubric for deciding how much time will be given to the various areas that require my attention, is love. Love shall be my guide. Love shall be my metal detector. Whatsoever things are love-wortny, will receive the bulk of my time today!

Today I am grateful for:

Introspective/Reflection Questions:

1. Name three family members whom you love, but haven't made enough time for lately?
2. Name three friends whom you lovem but haven't made enough time for lately?

GRATITUDE Journey

Homework:

Create your to do list with those names in mind. How can you spread love to those people who fill your love tank? Do something different today and tell them how much they mean to you. Life is too short. Don't put it off intil tomorrow.

51. LOVE SHALL GUIDE MY EVERY STEP

God is love, and without God there is nothing left. With that in mind, I will bring God into every moment of my day. God will guide my every step whether I'm walking, driving, flying, or riding. In my home, love shall guide me. At work, love shall guide me. When I'm alone, love will guide me. Every step I take today, I will remember to say "thank you for love. Thank you that I am loved. Thank you for loving me."

Today I am grateful for:

Introspective/Reflection Questions:

1. What is your favourite scripture about love?
2. What is your first memory of love in your life?

GRATITUDE *Journey*

Homework:

Today, find a song, a story, a sermon, or a scripture about love and meditate on it all day.

52. I WILL ALWAYS LET LOVE PRECEDE ME

God's banner over me is love. God loves me with an intentionality unlike any other. He always goes before me. He opens Red Seas. He dries the ground upon which I will walk. He tears down Jericho Walls. He makes my path straight. So I will not get in God's way. I will let God's love precede me. I will allow God to lead me and guide me in the path of righteousness for his name sake, and I will be grateful for every mountain and every valley along the way.

Today I am grateful for:

Introspective/Reflection Questions:

1. Name a time when you got in God's way.
2. Now recall a time when you let God take the lead.

53. WHAT ARE MY SIGNS OF LOVE?

Everything comes with a sign. There is a label for every product, and a clue for every mystery. The same is true for love. Love has signs. Love is patient. Love is kind. Love does not keep score. Love does not boast. As I think through this short list of love signs, I will choose gratitude for the people who really love me the way Christ loves the church. I will not spend time focusing on who does not love me; instead I will be grateful for those who do.

Today I am grateful for:

_____

_____

_____

_____

_____

_____

Introspective/Reflection Questions:

1. How can you be more patient today?
2. How can you be more kind today?

GRATITUDE Journey

_____

_____

_____

_____

_____

_____

_____

Homework:

During your devotional time today, Read 1 Corinthians 13 and pay attention to each attribute of love. Then quiz yourself by asking if you reflect the attributes described in that chapter. Be honest but also gentle with yourself. God is going to transform your inner love life today.

54. I CHOOSING LOVE FOR MYSELF AND EVERYONE AROUND ME

I will not let bitterness make me barren. I will not let their mistreatment of me turn me cold toward them. Instead, I will take the higher road. I will choose the narrower way. I will do what Christ did to his enemies. I will bless those who curse me and pray for those who use me. Most importantly, I will choose to love myself better than anyone can love me. For this disposition and conviction, I am grateful.

Today I am grateful for:

Introspective/Reflection Questions:

1. Name the last person who took advantage of you. List their initials below.
2. Name someone who has hurt your feelings in the near or distant past. List their initials below.

GRATITUDE Journey

Homework:

Take a moment today to pray for each person you listed above. Pray fervently. Intercede for them. Bless them and pray that God will make their dreams come true. This is how love grows up within us - when we can pray for those who have not prayed for us.

55. THE DEVIL IS A LIAR AND GOD IS PROMISE-KEEPER

The truth is God's lexicon. Everything he says will come to pass. And everything the devil says, is fiction. The lies may sound good, but I will not be deceived by good-sounding words. Instead, I will incline my ear to God's promises, and thank him for every word he has kept. He promised to keep my family—He kept his word. He promised to prosper me—He kept his word. He promised to heal me, and he has kept his word! Thank you!

Today I am grateful for:

Introspective/Reflection Questions:

1. What is a constant lie that devil has tried to make you believe?
2. How do you know it's a lie?

GRATITUDE Journey

Homework:

Today, every time the devil tries to bring a lie into your mind, replace it with a truth. Replace it with God's word. Reject the lie immediately and don't let it fester. You are loved. You are enough. You are the winner. You will get what God has for you. Anything outside that truth, is a lie.

56. I AM LEARNING TO BE CONTENT IN MY OWN SKIN

The world is full of beautiful people. The goal is not to compare myself to others, but to fully accept who I am, and how God made me. I'm not the average person on the video. I'm not the cookie cutter prototype that others may find beautiful enough. But God thinks I am to die for, and I am learning to be grateful for the skin I'm in, and content in the skin I'm in. I am enough.

Today I am grateful for:

Introspective/Reflection Questions:

1. Name a physical attribute that you love about yourself?
2. Name something that you used to dislike about you, but now you're learned to love it.

Homework:

It takes daily practice to love all of you. Today, allow the beauty of God's image through you to shine. Take a picture outside, find a good angle and some good light and spread your beautiful-ness to the world!

57. I AM CONTENT WITH WAITING

There is a blessing in the wait. There are hidden benefits in waiting. Because I know that good things come to those who wait, I will be grateful for every stage of this life. I am grateful for the process and not just the promise. I am grateful for the things I am learning while I'm waiting for what I need. This is going to be a wonderful moment in time, and I don't want to miss any of it. Therefore, I will learn to be content, and I will not rush this moment.

Today I am grateful for:

Introspective/Reflection Questions:

1. What are you waiting on relationally, and you are praying for God to make it happen?
2. What are you waiting on financially, and you are praying for God to make it happen?

GRATITUDE Journey

Homework:

As you wait, thank God for what He has already done. Make a list of miracles, signs, wonders, and moments where God has already come through for you - and as you wait for THOSE things, take a moment to appreciate THESE things.

58. I AM CONTENT WITH A DAY WELL LIVED

Every day is a day of thanksgiving, and to not be grateful, is to not live at all. Today, I will look for small ways to be grateful. I will focus on living well. I will slow down and pay attention. I will make room for intentional conversation. I will give a little more love today than I did yesterday.

Today I am grateful for:

Introspective/Reflection Questions:

1. Whad does it mean to "live well" in your own words?
2. According to the definition you just created, are you living well?

GRATITUDE Journey

Homework:

Think about the areas in which you are exelling. Now think about the areas in which you need improvement in order to live well. What major shift do you need to make in order to experience wellness and wholeness in your life. Begin a 3-day journey toward wellness, and make your wellness your top priority this week.

59. I SEE MY OWN VALUE AND WORTH

I am above and not beneath. I am the head and not the tail. I am valuable and I am worthy. I will not live beneath my standards. I will not settle for less than the best. When I am tempted to conform to the norm, I will remember that God made me peculiar. I am fearfully and wonderfully made, and I will remind myself of this truth, all day today.

Today I am grateful for:

Introspective/Reflection Questions:

1. Name a time when you settled.
2. Name a time when you "broke up" with the settling mentality.

GRATITUDE Journey

Homework:

Who inspires you to remember your value the most? Whose words minister to you and help you to realign? Listen to that person today. Whether it is in a person or on the internet. Find their words, and sit at their feet.

60. I SEE MYSELF ENJOYING LIFE TO THE FULLEST

Life is to be enjoyed. Love is to be embraced. Today, I will set an intention to enjoy my life. Yes, it could be better. Yes, I could have more money. Yes, I could have a newer home. But today, I will be thankful for what I have—for my health, for my strength, and for my family. Life is great, and I'm so grateful to be alive!

Today I am grateful for:

Introspective/Reflection Questions:

1. Whad is your favourite outfit to wear in this season (or your favourite shoes)?
2. What is a material possession that has significant value and personal meaning to you?

GRATITUDE *Journey*

Homework:

Do something tangible that shows appreciation for the blessings you currently have. Get a car wash. Wear an outfit that you love. Take your spouse out on a date. But appreciate what you already have even as you are aiming to achieve something great.

61. I SEE MYSELF ENJOYING PEACE

Conflict and chaos are commonplace. Life brings with it unexpected storms and winds. But, I will look to the hills from whence cometh my help. I will not just live a peaceful life, I will enjoy a peaceful life. This means, when storms come, I will speak these words, "Peace be still." I speak to the outer winds of this world, and I speak to the inner winds of my spirit, and I embrace peace all around me.

Today I am grateful for:

Introspective/Reflection Questions:

1. Name a current storm you are experiencing in your "outer world."
2. Name a current storm you are experiencing within. How will you allow peace to guide your spirit in spite of the storm?

GRATITUDE *Journey*

Homework:

What kind of scenery helps you to find peace? Is it the mountains, water, or the beautiful grass near your home? Find a place to go today that will help you to re-center your peace, and enjoy a short nap near nature.

62. I UNDERSTAND THE NEED FOR JUST 1 MINUTE

There are 365 days in a year. There are 24 hours in a day. Life is always moving. To Do lists seemingly never end. But sometimes, I just need one minute to inhale deeply and exhale completely. I will give myself a minute to fill my lungs with gratitude. I will realize that I have the power to control the pace of my day, and I will not be overwhelmed by life's pressures to rush into a frenzy. God is with me, and I will enjoy this one minute to say "Thank you."

Today I am grateful for:

Introspective/Reflection Questions:

1. Are you a morning person or a night owl?
2. When do you feel most centered?

Homework:

Find a time in the day to center yourself and breathe. Take 60 seconds and relax. Enjoy the moment for all it is worth. Don't allow any distractions to steal this moment of focus.

63. I AM THE BEST THING THAT GOD EVER CREATED

When God created the earth and the sky, he said "This is good." When God made the sea and the animals, he said, "This is good." But when God made me, he said "This is very good." I am God's very good creature. I am God's very best. I am, with confidence, the best thing that God ever created. I will live in the "very good" of God's best for me. I will not live beneath God's best for my life.

Today I am grateful for:

Introspective/Reflection Questions:

1. When do you feel at your best?
2. When do you feel at your worst?

GRATITUDE Journey

Homework:

Today do something that makes you feel your best. Go to the gym and break a personal goal. Go to the mall and purchase a well deserving gift. Do something for you, and remind yourself that you are VERY GOOD!

64. I AM A TRUE SOLDIER IN GOD'S ARMY

Paul wrote "I am a prisoner of Christ," and in the same way, I am a soldier in God's army. I enlist freely. I surrender completely. I would rather be a prisoner of Christ than to be a slave to my own choices. God's way is better. God's army gives protection. Today, I will choose to be grateful for the benefits of belonging to God's militant army.

Today I am grateful for:

Introspective/Reflection Questions:

1. What are some benefits to being enlisted in God's army?
2. What are some challenges as a result of being a part of God's army?

GRATITUDE Journey

Homework:

Today, make a decision to live a more disciplined life. Practice doing what you say you will do. Make a short list of three things you want to get done, and put a time frame around when you want to accomplish them. Then execute and celebrate once it's completed!

65. I AM SOMEBODY

God didn't make a mistake when he made me. God didn't duplicate his gifts when he created me. Everything he put inside me, he put it there for purpose and on purpose. My gifts, my skills, my emotions, my passions, all of it prove the uniqueness of my being. I am somebody. I am God's child. I am his choice prize. I am the treasure in his chest, and the spark in his eyes. Today, I will be grateful that God sees me as unique, and significant—and when others try to sway me, I will remember His promises over my life.

Today I am grateful for:

Introspective/Reflection Questions:

1. What are you passionate about?
2. What are you skillful in?

GRATITUDE Journey

Homework:

Today realize that you are an answer to a problem. Walk into every room with assurance that you are the person for the job. You are going to bring safety, security, comfort, and knowledge. Shine baby Shine!

66. I WILL DAILY PROCLAIM WHO I AM

I am who God says I am. I am royalty. I am divine. I am loyal. I am magnificent. I am a winner. I am a finisher. I am focused. I am beloved. Nothing shall hurt me. Nothing shall harm me. I am enough, because Christ died for me. I will live and not die, and these words I will proclaim today, all day, as I look in the mirror. Thank you Lord for new love and new vision.

Today I am grateful for:

Introspective/Reflection Questions:

1. What is one Christ-like trait that you aspire to embody more and more today?
2. What is one Christ-like trait that you already embody?

GRATITUDE Journey

Homework:

Today, listen to "Encourage Yourself" by Donald Lawrence and remind yourself that you are God's child.

67. I AM GOD'S ANOINTED GIFT

Gifts may cost a lot, but they are freely given. The Giver of the gift, then, places value in the product, and the process. I am God's great gift He has anointed me for purpose. He has crafted me with intentionality. Others may enjoy my wrapping paper, but there is more to me, and in me, than what you see. Today, I will find gratitude in the inner and outer gifts that make me, me!

Today I am grateful for:

Introspective/Reflection Questions:

1. What are you gifted to do?
2. How has that gift helped someone recently?

GRATITUDE Journey

Homework:

Today buy yourself a gift. It can be a gift from the dollar store, or a gift from Neiman Marcus. But after you buy the gift, take time to wrap it. As you wrap it, remind yourself that God has wrapped you as His gift for the world. As you enjoy the gift you purchased for yourself, remember to give yourself to someone today, intentionally!

68. I AM WORTHY OF EVERYTHING GOD HAS FOR ME

Perspective is everything. I am not a beggar. I am an heir. I am not beneath. I am above. Today, I remind myself to live on my level. I am worthy of what God has for me, and I will not be ashamed of who he says I am. I will shift my paradigm. I will enjoy every inch of my life. This is going to be a fantastic day, because everything I connect with, becomes better because I am a part of it.

Today I am grateful for:

Introspective/Reflection Questions:

1. What part of your life do you love the most?
2. What part of your life do you love the least? Can you see anything great about the most unlikeable part of your life?

Homework:

Create a gratitude wall and add to it each day. The goal is to find reasons to be grateful and encourage your family to do the same. The more grateful we are, the more God has room to bless us and blow our minds.

69. I KNOW MY GOD IS ABLE

Obstacles are opportunities. Barriers are breakthroughs. Despite the current situation I am enduring, I will give praise to God because I know God is able. God is able to heal. God is able to liberate. God will restore. God will renew. I am thankful for God's supernatural ability in the face of natural inability. Indeed, God is able!

Today I am grateful for:

Introspective/Reflection Questions:

1. What are you believing God for personally?
2. What are you believing God for relationally?

GRATITUDE Journey

Homework:

Find a scripture that speaks to God's sovereign ability. Post it on your social media page. Encourage a friend with it during lunch. Walk in that verse all day long, and cling to it until what you believe, manifests.

70. I WILL CHOOSE LOVE UNTIL IT BECOMES WHO I AM

Love is not just what I do. Love is who I am. Today, I choose to love people with the best in me. I choose to love people, especially when it is hard. I will choose to do as Christ did. I will give my life for others, because He gave his life for me.

Today I am grateful for:

Introspective/Reflection Questions:

1. Name a time when you had to love someone even though it was hard.
2. Name someone who is easy to love.

GRATITUDE Journey

Homework:

What does it mean to give your life for others? When is the last time you visited a homeless shelter or a home for the elderly? Can you find time this week to spread love in a place that may not receive much love?

71. I WILL REMEMBER TO SEIZE THE MOMENT

I am grateful for the time I have been given. I am grateful for the grace that has been extended. I will not let it pass. I will not be like the foolish servant who buried his talent. I will remember that the master is coming and I will have to give an account of what I did with the time I had. Today, I will be grateful for the time I have left, and I will do all I can to make the most of this moment.

Today I am grateful for:

Introspective/Reflection Questions:

1. What does grace mean to you?
2. Name a time when you missed an opportunity. How did it make you feel?

GRATITUDE Journey

Homework:

Encourage someone today not to miss their moment. Ask them what their dreams are, and then challenge them to pursue them. Volunteer yourself as their accountability partner and then check on them periodically over the next 3 months.

72. LOVE IS MY FIRST RESPONSE

Love is who I am. It is not just a part of me. It is my ontological reality. Therefore, I will not treat love as a last resort. Instead, love will be my first response. Love will be my "go-to" and my reflex. I will love in spite of. I will love because of. I will love others until they are fully able to love themselves.

Today I am grateful for:

Introspective/Reflection Questions:

1. Can you recall a moment when you didn't love yourself?
2. What was stopping you from self-love?

Homework:

Today, be someone's breath of fresh air. Compliment them on their outfit, or thank them for contributing to your organization. Go out of your way to give the kind of love you want to receive. Remember, we reap what we so.

73. PATIENCE IS MY FIRST RESPONSE

Because love is patient, I will embrace patience. Patience will be my first response. When I find myself annoyed, I will pause and pray for patience. I am thankful that God was patient with me during my prodigality and moments of wander. Therefore, I will be patient with others—especially with those in my family.

Today I am grateful for:

Introspective/Reflection Questions:

1. When was the last time you made a "BIG MISTAKE?"
2. Who is someone in your life that seems to make a lot of senseless mistakes? Why do you think they continue to repeat that behavior?

GRATITUDE Journey

Homework:

Today, take 5 minutes to pray for the person you mentioned above. Ask God to help them. Ask God to heal them. Ask God to transform their mind so that their actions can one day match their intentions.

74. I AM WOMAN, HEAR ME ROAR

I don't want to be anyone else but myself. I am a woman. I am righteous. I am special. I am unique. When I show up, answers show up. When I show up, solutions appear. I will not be afraid. I will be the lioness that God called me to be. I am woman, hear me roar! I am grateful for my confidence. I am grateful for my distinctiveness. Everything about me will be used to help others find freedom.

Today I am grateful for:

Introspective/Reflection Questions:

1. What is the best thing about being a woman?
2. What is the best thing about being you?

GRATITUDE Journey

Homework:

Today, take three pictures of yourself and post it on social media using the hashtag #I LIKE ME. Encourage your sisters and your friends to do the same. Let's start a LOVE MOVEMENT on SOCIAL MEDIA!

75. I AM AN EXAMPLE TO MY CHILDREN

Children are a gift from above. Because of that, I will lead my children to the Father. I will be an example to my biological children and to my spiritual children. Just like Eli was an example for Hannah's child, Samuel, I will be an example for others. I am grateful for the innocence that children bring to the world, and I will live upright before God and before them.

Today I am grateful for:

Introspective/Reflection Questions:

1. List all of your biological children below.
2. List all of your spiritual children below.

GRATITUDE Journey

Homework:

Call each of them today and speak something beautiful into their lives. You never know what your phone call will do for someone who may not be as excited about life today, as you are.

76. I AM AN EXAMPLE TO OTHERS

What a powerful privilege it is to be used by God. What an awesome opportunity it is to be His example. Today I will remember that everyone may not be a pastor, but everyone has a pulpit. That is to say, I may not be delivering a sermon from a platform, but my life is preaching a sermon every day. For this reason, I will walk in obedience. I will walk in surrender. I will be an example to others, the way Christ was an example for his disciples.

Today I am grateful for:

Introspective/Reflection Questions:
1. What sermon is your life preaching today?
2. How do you share your story with others?

Homework:
Today, use your platform (the beautician chair, the social media space, the radio, the lunchroom, a blog, etc) to share your story with the world. Encourage others to do the same, and make sure to spread gratitude for every part of your story.

77. I AM OUT OF THE BOX

God, the Father is a creator and I am too. I am innovative. I am abundantly blessed with ideas and strategies. The box was created to restrict and constrict others, but my creativity cannot be confined to a box. I am grateful today for my out-of-the-box perspective and personality. I will not allow others to box me in and restrain my thoughts. Instead, I will think big and dream far.

Today I am grateful for:

Introspective/Reflection Questions:

1. What makes you different?
2. How does your uniqueness reflect the beauty and diversity of God?

GRATITUDE *Journey*

Homework:

Create a box or purchase a box and then take a few markers and craft a drawing that always reminds you that you are OUT OF THE BOX. Share this activity with a group of friends or family members. For one day, embrace the inner child and use this project as a consistent sign of God's uniqueness in and through you.

78. SIMPLY, THANK YOU LORD

Gratitude is flowing from my heart today because God is good. Thank you, Lord, for waking me up this morning. Thank you, Lord, for starting me on my way. Thank you, Lord, for not allowing me to react in anger, but to respond with grace. Thank you that your grace is sufficient, and that I am enough.

Today I am grateful for:

Introspective/Reflection Questions:

1. Have you ever found yourself ungrateful? What caused you to think that way?
2. Have you ever heard "thank you" from an unexpected source? How did it make you feel.

GRATITUDE *Journey*

Homework:

Today come up with 21 reasons to Thank God! List them in the space provided on this page or in a journal. Title it "My Thank You Letter to God," and share it with others so they might be encouraged to do the same. Remember: a thank you never hurt anybody!

79. I AM GOING TO STAND UP AND DO SOMETHING

Injustice anywhere is injustice everywhere. Today I will both thank God for my freedom, and I will call out the injustice that I see in the world. I will raise my voice, come alongside the marginalized persons in this community and advocate for them. Everyone deserves justice and I am here to help others to live.

Today I am grateful for:

Introspective/Reflection Questions:

1. What is the last thing you saw on the news that broke your heart (as it relates to justice)?
2. How can you be an answer to a problem happening in your city?

GRATITUDE Journey

Homework:

Today, call someone who works as a police officer, a soldier, a veteran, a firefighter, or a political official and thank them for their service. Remember: a thank you goes a long way!

80. I SHALL RISE UP

God is looking for someone to rebuild the wall and stand in the gap. God is looking for someone to be an answer to someone's prayer. God is looking for someone to stand on the frontline and be the light in a dark world. He can trust me to do so. I will always be ready.

Today I am grateful for:

Introspective/Reflection Questions:

1. Identify a "dark" place in the world that needs your light.
2. What gifts, skills and talents can God use to help bring real solutions in the world today?

GRATITUDE Journey

Homework:

Today, look in your local newspaper for someone you can reach out to, to help in some small way. Email them and let them know that they are in your prayers. Don't forget to be the light in your community, and in your city. If you need direction, ask your pastor for a place to serve in the city that can bring real solutions and assistance to those in need.

81. GOD ALWAYS HAS THE FINAL SAY

No matter what my circumstances look like, I will remember that God knows what He is doing. He is working things out for my good. Fear cannot win. Darkness won't overtake me. The enemy I see today I will see no more because God is the author and the finisher of everything that concerns me.

Today I am grateful for:

Introspective/Reflection Questions:

1. Name a time when you thought God would not come through, but in the end, he did.
2. What are you currently hoping that God will do for you and your family? Name it and then write a prayer of faith below.

GRATITUDE Journey

Homework:

The prayer of faith will heal every sick thing in your life. Write a prayer of faith for your personal needs or the needs of your family. Trust God to supply all your needs according to his riches in glory. God is faithful that promised!

82. GOD IS USING ME FOR SOMETHING EXTRAORDINARY

God is doing something BIG and I am here for it. Not for my glory but for His. With a grateful heart, I say thanks. I give myself away so He can use me. Not just my talents and skills, but my story. I want my life to be a testimony of God's unending faithfulness and my gratitude to Him.

Today I am grateful for:

Introspective/Reflection Questions:

1. Reflect on a part of your story that you've never told anyone. How did God get the glory out of your story?
2. How can you share that story to someone who may need to hear it?

GRATITUDE *Journey*

Homework:

Today, look in your local newspaper for someone you can reach out to, to help in some small way. Email them and let them know that they are in your prayers. Don't forget to be the light in your community, and in your city. If you need direction, ask your pastor for a place to serve in the city that can bring real solutions and assistance to those in need.

83. I LOVE ME SOME ME

Flaws and all, I love me some me. Imperfections and shortcomings, I love me some me. Strengths and weaknesses, I love me some me. I am learning to embrace every part of my being and my existence— my wisdom and my wit; my joy and my jourtney. God has fashioned it all for His glory and I am grateful for this revelation. I am falling deeper and deeper in love with me.

Today I am grateful for:

Introspective/Reflection Questions:

1. What is something about you that you once saw as a flaw, but now you've come to embrace it?
2. What has embracing your flaws taught you about yourself, and about God?

GRATITUDE *Journey*

Homework:

Today, listen to the song "Flaws" by Kierra Sheard and share the lyrics with someone you love.

84. I LIKE WHAT I SEE WHEN I AM LOOKING AT ME

I used to be so hard on myself. I only saw flaws when I looked in the mirror. But after God changed my heart, I was able to see me the way He does. Now, I see a beautiful soul. Now I see a strong-willed leader. I am finally coming into my own, and I like what I see. Today, I'm thankful for a perspective shift.

Today I am grateful for:

Introspective/Reflection Questions:

1. How has your perspective changed over the last 10 years?
2. How have you matured over the last year?

Homework:

Today, take yourself out to eat, and treat yourself. Congratulate yourself for your growth, and enjoy this beautiful journey called LIFE.

85. I WILL LOVE REGARDLESS

I love God and myself enough to extend love even when I don't get it back. I have lived long enough to know that loving is a gift many do not experience. I am grateful for the gift of love; and I will not withhold it from anyone I encounter today.

Today I am grateful for:

Introspective/Reflection Questions:

1. Name someone who took advantage of your life (at one point in your life).
2. If you were to see that person today, what would you do? How would you feel?

GRATITUDE Journey

Homework:

Today, release yourself from any bitterness, pain, regret, remorse or sorrow. Life is about learning. The season is over. You have to move forward. Decide that you have cried your last tear, about this, yesterday. And once and for all, let it GO.

86. FORGIVENESS IS THE GREATEST PART OF SELF-LOVE

Give us this day our daily bread, and forgive us our debts as we forgive our debtors. I am grateful for the power of forgiveness. I am grateful for the journey of self-love. It has taken me years to learn what I know now, but I will give the gift of forgiveness to others because it is truly a gift to myself.

Today I am grateful for:

Introspective/Reflection Questions:

1. What is your favorite fruit?
2. What is your favorite flavor of ice cream?

Homework:

Today, buy yourself your favorite fruit and your favorite flavor of ice cream as a reminder that every time you forgive, you pour love back into yourself. As you enjoy your delicious snacks, thank God for the season you were in, and thank God for the season he brought you out of!

87. OBSTACLES ARE MY DISGUISED STEPPING STONES

Just like James 1 teaches, I will rejoice and be glad when I face obstacles, trials and tribulations. They are developing something in me. They are taking me higher. Obstacles are taking me to my next level. So today, I am thankful for my obstacles because every obstacle has the potential to become an opportunity.

Today I am grateful for:

Introspective/Reflection Questions:

1. What are present obstacles that you are facing in your life professionally, emotionally, and financially?
2. Name a time when something you thought was an obstacle, actually became an opportunity? How did it develop you?

GRATITUDE Journey

Homework:

The only way to face these obstacles is to choose not to ignore them. Consult someone you trust and discuss each obstacle until you come up with a plan to face it and defeat it. Don't stop talking about it until the plan is clear and the adjustments are made. You can do this!

88. STICK-TO-ITIVENESS IS MY GIFT TO ME

I will not drop the ball. I will not start something I cannot complete. When life becomes overwhelming, I will reach down, breath deeply, and get it done. I have everything I need to complete it. I have the ideas. I have the funds, and I have the stick-to-itiveness to keep going when the excitement disappears. This is a gift I give to myself, and I will remember this moment when it's done!

Today I am grateful for:

Introspective/Reflection Questions:

1. Why is the goal, you are trying to reach, so hard today?
2. How do you conquer feelings of defeat when you no longer feel like going on?

Homework:

When goals become really difficult, sometimes you need a day to just rest. Don't beat yourself up. Take a commercial break. Back up from the project. Release yourself from the need to fix it, and decide "I'll handle this tomorrow."

89. I WILL STAY THE COURSE

It's always hard until it's done. Therefore, I press toward the mark and I commit to staying the course. I will speak what I seek until I see what I spoke. I will not waver. God is the author and the finisher of my faith. I am grateful for the assurance that if I stay this course, a greater reward is waiting for me.

Today I am grateful for:

Introspective/Reflection Questions:

1. What is something you want to finish within the next 30 days?
2. What is something you want to complete within the next 6 months?

GRATITUDE Journey

Homework:

Start a FINISHERS plan. Use the next 30 days as a litmus test. Decide what your goal is, then create action items that will help you to achieve it. Start with a small and realistic goal, and then work toward more challenging goals as you win, little by little.

90. TODAY, I CELEBRATE ME

God must've been showing off when he made me. I am winning. I am learning. I am trying new things. I am cherishing the memories of old. I celebrate how far I've come. I honor my growth. I have so much to be thankful and grateful for, and celebration is appreciation in disguise.

Today I am grateful for:

Introspective/Reflection Questions:

1. What is something you cherish from childhood that you wish you still could do?
2. What is something you've learned to do recently, that you took a risk to learn? Maybe it's a food you tried or a new hobby you picked up.

GRATITUDE Journey

Homework:

This month, create a list of 3 new things you want to do, and 3 old things you want to revive from your past. If you used to ride a bike but you don't have time for it now, make time. If you've never had sushi, try it! You may actually like it! The goal is to be grateful for the past, the present, and the future!

91. I AM CHALLENGING MYSELF TO LET GO

I am letting go of everything that does not serve me anymore. I am shedding old mindsets and discarding unnecessary patterns of thought. I am letting go of toxic friendships and family ties that hold me back from thriving. I am unlearning that the unhealthy coping mechanisms that I picked up from childhood, no longer serve me well. I am not who I used to be. Therefore, I am grateful for the "let go."

Today I am grateful for:

Introspective/Reflection Questions:

1. What do you need to let go of in this chapter of your life? Why?
2. Who do you need to let go of in this chapter of your life? Why?

GRATITUDE *Journey*

Homework:

Letting go is not easy to do. Often, we need a "pros and cons" list to compare and contrast why we are letting go of a certain thing or a certain person. Create your pros and cons list so that, when you find yourself rethinking your decision, you have something to reference.

92. I GIVE MYSELF PERMISSION TO LIVE

Now that I let it all go, I give myself permission to live. Not just to live, but to thrive. Christ died to give us abundant life and I want to experience God's best for my life. After all I have been through, I will live to testify to the work of the Lord.

Today I am grateful for:

Introspective/Reflection Questions:

1. If you could live wherever you wanted to live, where would it be?
2. If you could do something spectacular with your life, what would it be?

GRATITUDE Journey

Homework:

Design a plan to actualize your dreams. Nothing is too hard for God. But first you have to admit what you want to do. Dare to dream and see what comes of it.

93. I GIVE MYSELF PERMISSION TO FORGIVE

Now that I have let it all go, I give myself permission to forgive. Unforgiveness is the only prison cell that locks and unlocks the victim inside, from the inside. Forgiveness is a gift often given to others but rarely to ourselves. Today, I choose to forgive myself for the mistakes I made along the way. I am forgiving myself for the choices I made when I did not know any better. I learned the lesson; therefore I can graduate.

Today I am grateful for:

Introspective/Reflection Questions:

1. Do you beat yourself up for things God has forgiven you for?
2. Do you struggle with self blame and discouragement? Where does that come from?

GRATITUDE *Journey*

Homework:

Record a voice note to your younger self. Tell her what you wish you had known when you were her age. Forgive her for the mistakes of her past and give her permission to move on. After you finish recording it, listen to it and receive your own healing from your own voice.

94. HOW BAD DO I WANT WHAT GOD HAS FOR ME?

I am grateful today for zeal and commitment. I am committed to going full throttle after everything God wants for me. He knows what is best for me. He knows what my highest calling is. He will lead me toward my prize, and give me the desire for what He desires.

Today I am grateful for:

Introspective/Reflection Questions:

1. What do you believe your calling is? How do you know?
2. If everyone has a calling, then everyone also has a higher calling. Have you ever thought about what your higher calling is?

GRATITUDE Journey

Homework:

Think about the ultimate gift you bring to the world. Think about the ultimate gift you bring to your family. Now what would you do if someone gave you one million dollars, and then gave you permission to walk in your calling? What would you start and more importantly, what would you stop? Design this plan under a 5-year strategy. Then pray and ask God to make it happen.

95. I WON'T TALK ABOUT IT, I WILL BE ABOUT IT

I refuse to just talk a good game and post about my plans. I will focus on follow-through. I will make more moves and less announcements. Because I know that faith without works is dead, then I accept that "talk alone" won't get me where I need to be. I am choosing gratitude for the determination and execution necessary to complete what I've started.

Today I am grateful for:

Introspective/Reflection Questions:

1. Would you say that you "talk about plans" better than you "execute" them? Why or why not?
2. Would your friends say you are a DOER, A THINKER, or a PLANNER?

GRATITUDE Journey

Homework:

Instead of crafting a to do list of things you will accomplish this week, come up with one task that you will do each day, and set a goal to do that! After a week, see if you were able to follow-through on smaller, less extensive lists. It may help you focus!

96. I AM ROYALTY

Every day, I become more keenly aware of who I am in God. Every moment, I am taking more seriously the way God sees me, and how I should reflect his perspective of me and not my own. I am a child of the most high God. I am a co-heir with Christ. I am not at the bottom of the totem pole. I am God's masterpiece. Therefore, I will thank God for every person, place or thing which has come into my life to remind me of my royal status in God's eyes.

Today I am grateful for:

Introspective/Reflection Questions:

1. Have you always been secure in light of who God says you are?
2. How might you encourage other women to find security and boldness in their identity?

GRATITUDE Journey

Homework:

If you could come up with a reality show about beauty, image, identity, and security in faith, what would it be? What would you call it? How would the women help others to increase their confidence and better align with their faith? Just for fun, design a reality show that centers around royalty, and share it with your spiritual leader or the pastor's wife.

97. I AM OPENING MY SELF-INFLICTED PRISON BARS

I am running out of the jail I put myself in. I am leaving behind my pain, my past, and the poison of a self-inflicted prison. I am not my mistakes. I am not my failures. I am better. I am stronger, and I am choosing to prosper in gratitude. God has given me another day to change my trajectory, and I'm going to win!

Today I am grateful for:

Introspective/Reflection Questions:

1. What are some invisible bars you have placed yourself in, in the past?
2. How did you break free from that mindset.

GRATITUDE *Journey*

Homework:

Everything begins with grateful. Today, list all of the things God freed you from, and after you list them, write the word "thank you." As we mature in Christ, we learn to give thanks IN all things even when we can't give thanks FOR all things.

98. I LIKE WHO I AM BECOMING ON THIS JOURNEY

The fruit of the Spirit is evident in my life. God has started a good work in me and He will complete it. I like who I am becoming. I like who God has made me. This journey has taught me that God makes no mistakes. God uses everything for his glory, and for my good; and for this, I am grateful!

Today I am grateful for:

Introspective/Reflection Questions:

1. What is one good thing that came out of this week for you?
2. What is one great thing about you, that was only developed after adversity and difficulty.

Homework:

Meditate on Galatians 5:22-23 and list the fruit of the spirit. Circle the areas where you may be strong in (love, joy, etc), and then underline the areas where you need God to continue to work on you (patience, temperance, etc.).

99. WHAT IS MY FAITH CALLING INTO EXISTENCE?

God gives me the power to speak those things that are not as though they were. So, to the poor, I am rich. To the weak, I am strong. To the sick, I am healed. To the overwhelmed, I am clear. To the shackled, I am free. Today I am joyfully excited about my ability to speak life into every dead situation, and I commit to doing so all day long!

Today I am grateful for:

Introspective/Reflection Questions:

1. What area in your life needs like spoken into it today?
2. What loved one needs a little more encouragement today, than usual?

GRATITUDE *Journey*

Homework:

Spend 5-10 minutes praying with concentration for the person you named above, and the area that is lacking in your own life. Pray that God would lift burdens, heal hearts, and bring fresh faith into every weak and dry place. Pray until something happens. Pray until you feel lighter. Don't let go until God blesses you!

100. PUT A PRAISE ON IT AND GET WHAT YOU DESIRE

I praise God in advance for the blessing that is on the way. God is in control of the heavenly mail that is sent to my address. So even though it has not been delivered to my home, I will praise Him in advance as a sign of my trust in Him. I believe God will not withhold any good thing from those who love him, and I truly love him! Therefore, I commit to making room for the explosive blessings of God!

Today I am grateful for:

Introspective/Reflection Questions:

1. What is one non-materialistic blessing that you are believing God for?
2. What is something that you hope God will do for someone close to you?

GRATITUDE Journey

Homework:

There are many ways to praise God. Some sing. Some shout. Others write. Others dance. Today, carve out 20 minutes of your day to solely focus on praising God. Express gratitude to him for what He has done, and for what He will do. Go ahead! Praise Him!

101. I AM A QUEEN OF THE KINGDOM

I am royalty. I am honored. I am worthy of God's best. I am an heir of God's throne. I am his Queen. When people see me today, they will see my Father in heaven. Through my reflection, they will know that he lives in me. I am grateful that I am not an orphan. I am not alone. I am a part of God's family, and because I belong to him, he is responsible for me.

Today I am grateful for:

Introspective/Reflection Questions:

1. What does it mean, to you, to be a Queen of the Kingdom?
2. What are some attributes of a queen that differ from a slave?

GRATITUDE *Journey*

Homework:

Today, take time to study the Queen of England. Study her apparel. Listen to her speak. Do a little bit of research (maybe 10 minutes only) on how she maneuvers through life. Aim to mirror what you have learned in your own life, and watch how differently people will treat you, once you finally see yourself through the lens of Royalty.

102. BREATHE AND BE

Everyone wants to be somewhere, but the best place to be, is right where we are. In this moment, I will not worry about tomorrow because today has enough troubles of its own. I won't rush through the day. I will stop and smell the roses. I will embrace the tension I feel. I will be present with God, the people that I love and with myself. Thank You for breath in my body. I will BE and BREATHE. BREATHE and BE.

Today I am grateful for:

Introspective/Reflection Questions:

1. When is the last time you paused to do nothing? Do you struggle with stillness?
2. How do you calm your mind when worry or anxiety is invading your thoughts?

GRATITUDE Journey

Homework:

Tear out a sheet a paper from a notebook. Write down everything you are worried about. Write down all the responsibilities you have, the bills you need to pay; write down whatever is weighing you down. Then crumble up that paper, and pray over it. Ask God to take your pressure and your worry, and when you say Amen, rip up that paper into little shreds. Pay attention to what happens in your body when you release it.

103. I AM DETERMINED TO LIVE MY LIFE

My life will not unravel by chance. My decisions will not happen accidentally. I am determined to live my life on purpose, and in purpose. I will be grateful for each opportunity, and I will not cruise through life's journey in neutral. Instead, I will press onto the high gears of this beautiful experience God has given me, and I will invite others to do the same. Life without joy is no life at all! Therefore, I choose JOY.

Today I am grateful for:

Introspective/Reflection Questions:

1. What is the best thing that happened to you an hour ago?
2. What is the best thing that happened to you a minute ago?

GRATITUDE Journey

Homework:

Determination requires concentration. Today, block out all the noise—drive in the car with no music or distractions. Use your commute time to think about what you will do differently today, as a sign that you are living life. Experiment with something you've never tried before. Surprise yourself. You just may learn something about yourself that you didn't know existed.

104. MY PRISON DOORS ARE OPEN

Life now is sweet and my joy is complete. Everything that once confined me and defined me, is over. All of the sorrow has been converted to joy. My mourning has transformed into dancing. My prison doors are open and I am ready to embrace my newfound freedom. Today is a day of complete liberation from people's opinions, thoughts, and agenda. God has made me free and I will remain free!

Today I am grateful for:

Introspective/Reflection Questions:

1. Have you ever been in a confined space and could not get out? How did that make you feel?
2. What new thing can you do today to honor your freedom?

GRATITUDE *Journey*

Homework:

Freedom is a beautiful word. Prison is a container and a place of confinement. Think about those who are in prison today, and pray for their wellbeing and their families. Pray that God will keep them in perfect peace, and that they will receive justice and mercy in this season.

105. WHAT AM I DREAMING ABOUT?

My dreams become my reality. My reality becomes my new normal. My new normal can build a path for others to follow. Whatever I dream, I can do. Therefore, I pay attention to what I'm dreaming about. And when I wake up, I will move into execution. I will move into action. I want my life to mean something, and I am determined to make it happen.

Today I am grateful for:

Introspective/Reflection Questions:

1. What are you thinking about? Are your thoughts producing actions that you are pleased with?
2. What are you dreaming about? Are these dreams leading you to the life you want to live?

GRATITUDE Journey

Homework:

During your quiet time, meditate on this quote about dreams: Dreams aren't what you leave behind when morning comes. They are the stuff that fill your every living moment – David Cuschieri

106. WHAT AM I DOING WITH MY TIME?

Time is so crucial. It is one of the single most important investments of our lives. Money, we can squander and gain back. Relationships, we can repair after confrontation or difficulty. Jobs can be given again. But our time is uniquely different. Once we lose it we can never gain it back. Today, I will thank God for my time. I will treasure and honor my time by only investing in things that matter.

Today I am grateful for:

Introspective/Reflection Questions:

1. What have you wasted time doing before that you want to stop doing today?
2. How can you honor your time a little better this week?

GRATITUDE Journey

Homework:

Create a "week in review" schedule. Write down everything you need to accomplish this week, and then assign a time to it. Give yourself margin so that you don't overcommit and under-produce. Then, evaluate how this practice helped you to honor your time in a different way.

107. I AM A CHILD OF GOD, A BRANCH OF THE TRUE VINE

Without God, I can do nothing. Without my Heavenly Father, I know I would fail. I am so grateful to be called His own. I am grateful that I have His DNA. I am grateful that when I cry, he is there to pick me up. I am a branch of the true vine. This means, I am connected to power. I am connected to protection. I am connected to provision.

Today I am grateful for:

Introspective/Reflection Questions:

1. Reflect on the last time God protected you from unexpected calamity. What happened and how did it shift your gratitude?
2. Recall a moment when God provided for you? How did that invigorate your understanding of being connected to Him?

GRATITUDE Journey

Homework:

All connections are not God connections. Today, think about your connections. Write down the top 5 people you talk to every day, and answer this question: are they connected to the Vine? If they are not, do I need to disconnect from them for a season.

108. MY NEXT LEVEL REQUIRES HOLINESS

Holiness is a beautiful picture of God's grace. Holiness reminds me that something in life is pure. Something in life is reserved for special use. In the same way, I must remember that God has made me special. I cannot give myself away without counting up the cost. Therefore, I will remember that holiness and gratitude go hand-in-hand. I will be intentionally grateful for the uniqueness that God created when he made me, and also the special and sacred space that God reserves for just me.

Today I am grateful for:

Introspective/Reflection Questions:

1. In your own words, what does holiness mean to you?
2. How might being more selective help you to cherish your body, soul, and mind?

GRATITUDE *Journey*

Homework:

Today think on these things. Think on pure things. Think on sacred things. Think on lovely things. Remove all unnecessary thoughts, and when distractions rush into your mind, refresh your mental space and return to holy and thankful thoughts.

109. TODAY IS THE BEGINNING OF EVERYTHING I EVER WANTED

I am so thankful for a new day! I am thankful for new beginnings. It's a season of power and prosperity. It's a season of renewal and restoration. Today, I will begin to appreciate the fact that God loves me enough to give me another chance. I will maximize on this moment and attract everything I ever wanted, by the words I say and the joy I spread.

Today I am grateful for:

Introspective/Reflection Questions:

1. If you could re-design your life, and start from scratch, what would you want to do with the rest of your life?
2. How will you maximize the greatness that is packed into the next 24 hours!?

GRATITUDE Journey

Homework:

Today, listen to the song "The Best Days of Your Life" by The Potter's House of Denver, and enjoy the lyrics and the upbeat tempo! It's going to be a GREAT DAY!

110. WHO AM I AND WHAT DO I WANT IN MY LIFE?

I am a woman of valor. I am a woman of strength. I am the head and not the tail. I am above and not beneath. I am beautifully and wonderfully made. Wisdom is my portion. I am in control of my life. God is my leader and I will follow him wholeheartedly. Today, I will be grateful for who I am and whose I am.

Today I am grateful for:

Introspective/Reflection Questions:

1. Here is a simple thing to reflect on today: What do YOU want in your life?
2. What don't you want in your life? How will you begin to eliminate what you don't want so that you can embrace what you do want?

GRATITUDE *Journey*

Homework:

Now that you've answered that simple question, does your life reflect more of what you want or don't want? How can you change that? Today, consider talking to a therapist or a close friend who can help you de-clutter your life so that there are more WANT TO's than DON'T WANT TO's going on in your life.

111. I AM A WOMAN OF TRANSFORMATION

I have learned that modification and transformation are similar but different. Modification is like cleaning a house. Transformation is like buying new furniture. Modification is like getting a make-over. Transformation is like exercising consistently until you don't look like what you've been through. Today, I am thankful for my life; and I will express gratitude for it by choosing not to settle for mere modification when I can have an amazing transformation!

Today I am grateful for:

Introspective/Reflection Questions:

1. Name something in your life that represents modification.
2. Name something in your life that represents transformation. How can you tell the difference?

GRATITUDE *Journey*

Homework:

Today, take a little time to YouTube "butterflies." Learn about their metamorphosis process and figure out a way to model your life after the transformation process. Write down what you learned, and share it with a friend.

112. I WILL NEVER GET IN MY OWN WAY

Today I am getting out of the driver's seat. I will stop acting like I know better than Him. I willingly submit to the process, knowing that He knows best. I submit my will and my intuition to Him. I do not want to make any decision that is not in line with His plan for me. I will NOT get in my own way.

Today I am grateful for:

Introspective/Reflection Questions:

1. What happened the last time you got in your own way? What did it teach you?
2. Can you think of a time when you trusted God to lead and guide you? What was the result?

GRATITUDE Journey

Homework:

Reflect on this chorus from the song "Jesus Take the Wheel" Today:

Jesus, take the wheel
Take it from my hands
'Cause I can't do this on my own
I'm letting go

So give me one more chance
And save me from this road I'm on
Jesus, take the wheel

113. NOTHING WILL PREVENT ME FROM FLYING HIGH

Today, I am taking the limits off of God and the plans he has for me. I am convinced that nothing can stop me from reaching my greatest potential. I am alive. I am alert. The Holy Spirit is the wind beneath my wings. If God is for me, then, nothing can stop me.

Today I am grateful for:

Introspective/Reflection Questions:

1. Why do you think we put limits on God?
2. Most people are afraid of heights in the literal sense. Are you afraid of heights, spiritually? If so, why?

GRATITUDE *Journey*

Homework:

Gather some friends at your home, or on facetime, and have a LIMITLESS Party? Ask them to craft their life without limits and do something that memorializes this moment.

114. I WILL ASK GOD FOR WHAT I WANT/DESIRE

If you're a parent, then you know that babies can be beautiful, but they can also be a burden. What do I mean? There's nothing more frustrating than a screaming baby and a parent not knowing why. I'm sure, if the baby could articulate their needs, they would...and the parent would be more than happy to oblige. God is the same way with us. He's ready to meet our needs, all we have to do is ask! He doesn't want us to hurt or to go lacking. He wants to provide and care for us. Therefore, I will no longer be ashamed and timid. I will ask God for everything I need AND desire. You should, too.

Today I am grateful for:

Introspective/Reflection Questions:

1. What are some basic desires that you have?
2. Have you ever felt ashamed or guilty for asking God to supply your basic needs? Why or why not?

GRATITUDE Journey

Homework:

Today list five needs you have and pray over each one. Your needs may range from emotional needs, physical needs, relational needs, or practical needs. Decide that you will not be ashamed to ask God to meet your needs. Why? Because he is faithful to supply all of our needs according to his riches in glory.

115. I MUST CREATE A QUIET SPACE IN MY LIFE

When life gets noisy, quiet time is mandatory. I've realized that the longer I live, the louder life gets. When things get loud, I will get quiet. When I experience quiet time with God, God has a way of drowning out the noise to allow me to hear exactly what I need to hear. Life goes on. They will be fine without me for two minutes of quiet time. Instead of waiting for people to give it to me, I will create it. Designating quiet time is like creating a blank canvas for destiny...literally anything can happen.

Today I am grateful for:

Introspective/Reflection Questions:

1. When is the last time you sat in quietness for more than 5 minutes?
2. What do you do to "center" yourself?

GRATITUDE *Journey*

Homework:

Today, take 5-10 minutes to be still and quiet. Find a "center" place. Disconnect and unplug from any distractions—phone, social media, noise, etc.—and experience what happens when you still your mind, body, and soul.

116. I WILL TREASURE THE QUIET SPACE CREATED IN MY LIFE

I remember my favorite jacket when I was a little girl. Some of my friends, classmates, and cousins would ask to try it on, but every time they'd ask, the answer would always be the same...nope! This is my jacket and I love it! I treasured that jacket, and I treasured my quiet space too. I will always hold dear that which fuels me. The quiet space that was created was for me. I value it.

Today I am grateful for:

Introspective/Reflection Questions:

1. What material possession do you value? Why?
2. How do you protect what you value? How can we protect our peace the way we protect our possessions?

GRATITUDE Journey

Homework:

Stillness has become an endangered species. Today, take back your peace and command your soul to be still and know that God is God. See calmness as a treasure and commit to protecting it with everything you have within you.

117. IF I KEEP THE FAITH, IT WILL ALWAYS WORK FOR ME

Faith is loyal. It enters the unseen and advocates on our behalf. It faces giants and tells them "I will not be defeated." It looks at mountains and says, "one of us has to move and it isn't me." Faith grows. Faith transforms. If I hold onto it, it'll always work for me. When I doubt and let it go, I'm on my own. Every time I've been on my own, it didn't work out so well. Therefore, I will be grateful for faith and I'll stick with faith from here on out.

Today I am grateful for:

Introspective/Reflection Questions:

1. What are you believing God for?
2. Name a time when "believing God" really worked out for you.

GRATITUDE *Journey*

Homework:

Today is testimony service day. Go on Facebook live and share with the world something that God has done for you. Or, post your testimony on social media and encourage someone you know or don't know, to keep the faith! We overcome by the blood of the lamb and by the words of our testimony.

118. NO MORE EXCUSES, I AM RUNNING WITH MY VISION

For years I didn't think I was good enough. Have you ever felt that? I'd convince myself that I needed to be a little smarter, change my appearance, or be in a different body to be great. Not this time. Enough is enough. I've wrote the vision. I believe it. Now, I'm running with it for my life. Laces tied.

Today I am grateful for:

Introspective/Reflection Questions:

1. What has been one excuse that has kept you stuck in life?
2. What can you tangibly do to circumvent that excuse today?

Homework:

Sometimes we need accountability partners in order to "run with our vision." Today, pick two people and ask them to join you on an accountability journey. Share with them your vision and ask them to share theirs as well. Together, come up with a plan to check in with each other on a weekly or monthly basis. Best of all, celebrate one another when the vision has been accomplished.

119. I AM NOT A REPEAT OFFENDER

Today I've decided to change. Most people think that breaking bad habits will take an Act of God or Congress to happen. I say, it all begins with a decision. A declaration. I've decided in my mind that I want to change. My habits are changing, my decisions are changing, and therefore, my life is changing. I might have done the deed, but "IT" is not who I am, and it is not who YOU are. I am not a repeat offender. Today, I am changed.

Today I am grateful for:

_____

_____

_____

_____

_____

_____

Introspective/Reflection Questions:

1. What makes change so difficult? What/Who means the most to you right now?
2. What can you do to ensure that you will not become a repeat offender in the area that means the most to you right now?

GRATITUDE *Journey*

_____

_____

_____

_____

_____

_____

_____

Homework:

Come up with a daily declaration that will focus your day. Repeat that declaration for the next 7 days. Write the declaration in the space provided on this page.

120. I NOW DANCE IN THE RAIN WITH PURPOSE

I used to run to escape the rain, but now I dance in the rain with purpose. Many of us loathe the idea of rain. It cancels outings, spoils barbecues, and forces you to seek shelter. However, rain also aids in bringing life to vegetation, it rinses the dirt and debris from roadways, and washes away all that needs refreshing. If the rain waters the seed, then when it rains, I'll be watered too; so why not dance? I refuse to see the storms of life as a negative. Instead, I will embrace them as the watering of seeds that I've sown. I will no longer run from the rain, now I'll dance in it...ON PURPOSE.

Today I am grateful for:

Introspective/Reflection Questions:

1. What does purpose mean to you?
2. Can you honestly say you are walking in purpose?

Homework:

Today listen to "Purpose Driven Life" by Melinda Watts and highlight the verse or line that speaks to you. Let it be a reminder to walk in your purpose every day—even if it rains.

121. I NOW SING WITH A PURPOSE

Over and over, the Bible instructs us to sing a new song. If the winds blow and the waves roar to declare God's goodness, then when I open my mouth, I pledge to do the same. When I speak I will glorify Him and when I sing, I will glorify him. I will sing with passion, with praise, and with purpose. Try it and watch how good you feel.

Today I am grateful for:

Introspective/Reflection Questions:

1. What's your favorite song currently?
2. What's an "oldie but goodie" that still brings you joy?

GRATITUDE Journey

Homework:

Today, take some time to make a playlist of songs that bring you joy. Show gratitude by smiling and inhaling and exhaling. Enjoy the songs. Zone out for a moment; and SMILE!

122. I CELEBRATE LOVING ME

There was a time in my life where I thought it was wrong to put me first. Everyone would always ask me (whether consciously or unconsciously) to place their priorities before my own, and I'd humbly say, "I don't mind", or "that's what Jesus would do." Little did I know, how I felt about myself showed in how I treated myself. Today I have decided to celebrate loving me. I am fearfully and wonderfully made, and it is okay to put me first. After all, that's what Jesus did. Think about it.

Today I am grateful for:

Introspective/Reflection Questions:

1. What is one thing you absolutely LOVE about yourself?
2. What is something you can do today that helps you to remember to celebrate self-love?

GRATITUDE Journey

Homework:

Whatever you answered in question number 2, do that today! Take yourself out to eat. Enjoy your favorite dessert. Indulge in a perfect manicure and pedicure. Book that quick getaway. Take a few selfies in the dress you haven't worn out the house yet. CELEBRATE YOU TODAY!

123. I AM BOLD, I AM CONFIDENT, I AM FREE

Each of us has a dual nature. The LION and the LAMB. Depending on the circumstances, the one you get that day may differ. I am not ashamed of that. One teaches me to be vigilant and go after what's mine, while the other reminds me of what I don't deserve that grace awards. Either way, I'm grateful. I'm bold, I'm confident, and I'm free. I can be a lion when I need to and a lamb when I'm supposed to. I'm blessed.

Today I am grateful for:

Introspective/Reflection Questions:

1. What emboldens you? Who empowers you?
2. When are you most confident?

GRATITUDE Journey

Homework:

Some of us are most confident after we get our hair done. Others of us are confident once we complete a project or make a perfect meal. Whatever brings you confidence and joy, do that today. Be unapologetically fearless and courageous. This is going to be a great day!

124. I HAVE MY WINGS, NOW IT'S TIME TO FLY

What if I told you that everything you need is already inside of you? Every business idea, every book, every strategy, it's all in you. We sometimes go our whole lives waiting for the "big bang" to come along and change everything, when the tools to change have been embedded within. I have what I need, I have my wings, now it's time to fly. Do it!

Today I am grateful for:

Introspective/Reflection Questions:

1. Has fear ever tried to clip your wings? When did you feel most afraid in your life, and why?
2. How did you break free from that fear? What did you do and who did you talk to?

GRATITUDE Journey

Homework:

Today, listen to Joyce Meyer's sermon titled "I will not fear." Youtube it and share it with a friend. It will bless your entire life.

125. I AM IN TOUCH WITH MY FEELINGS

The best thing you can say is "I love me." Be okay with where you are...or aren't. Be secure in what you can do and comfortable with what you can't. I know who I am, I know how I am, and I'm in touch with my feelings. They don't control me, they show me. They show me where I am and what I need... today. Each day we can begin again. Embrace that.

Today I am grateful for:

Introspective/Reflection Questions:

1. Before you started reading this entry, what were you feeling?
2. After you complete the homework assignment for today, write down what you are NOW feeling.

GRATITUDE *Journey*

Homework:

Take a moment to pray and examine your emotions. Sit still and ask yourself "how am I feeling? Why am I feeling this? How can I feel better?" After answering those questions, make it a priority to heighten and elevate your feelings today.

126. PHYSICIAN, HEAL THYSELF

You've been blessed with the gift of "Know How!" You know how it feels, you know how it hurts, and you know where it hurts. You've done the work, thoroughly examined the diagnosis, and now...it's time to be whole. Don't wait for others to fix you. Physician, heal thyself. You know how! You know what you have to do. Do it!

Today I am grateful for:

_____

_____

_____

_____

_____

_____

Introspective/Reflection Questions:

1. What does wholeness look like to you?
2. Can you think back to a time when you felt most whole? Who were you with, where did you live, what was happening in your life?

GRATITUDE Journey

_____

_____

_____

_____

_____

_____

_____

Homework:

If you feel further from that place of wholeness (based on the answer you gave in question #two), carve out a plan to get back to that place. Who do you need to forgive? Who do you need to release? Who do you need to apologize to? Where do you need to live? What do you need to let go of? Answering these questions will bring you back to healing and wholeness.

127. MY ABC'S ~ ADMIT IT, BREATHE, GET COUNSEL

Since our youth we've based our entire educational foundation on the elementary principles of the ABC's. Getting over trying times or heartbreak can be just as principled. As a result, try these foundational principles the next time you're struggling: Admit It, Breathe, and get Counsel. The only way to go is up!

Today I am grateful for:

Introspective/Reflection Questions:

1. What do you need to admit and then forget?
2. Who do you receive counsel from in this chapter of your life?

GRATITUDE Journey

Homework:

This week, schedule a 60-minute meeting with your counselor. This person may be a licensed clinician/therapist, your pastor, or a trusted friend. Either way, make your life priority and talk through what you've been carrying this week.

128. I HAVE POWER, LOVE, AND A SOUND MIND

Today, I refuse to give in to what I feel. Oftentimes we let our weaknesses convince us of a false reality. You may not feel blessed, but you are. You may not feel like smiling, but your smile does matter. You may feel weak, but really, you are strong. Say this, "I have power. I have love. I have a sound mind!" Declare it!

Today I am grateful for:

Introspective/Reflection Questions:

1. In what ways do you see power manifesting in your life today? Congratulate yourself after you name it.
2. Who do you need to show a little more love to, today? Be intentional about connecting with that person (even if that person is you).

GRATITUDE Journey

Homework:

Revisit the declaration you wrote a few weeks ago. Repeat it until you believe it! Remember, death and life are in the power of our tongue. The more we speak life, the more life we will receive and experience!

129. I AM GOING TO BE ABOUT MY WORK

When something belongs to you, we have the tendency to treat it better than how we'd treat other people's things. Furthermore, we expect others to treat our things as we would. Instead of giving everyone and everything else your best, give your business your best. This week I've decided to be about my work. Emphasis on "MY". We give some much attention to the things of others, that we limit what we have left for our business. Choose you today. Handle your business.

Today I am grateful for:

Introspective/Reflection Questions:

1. What personal business do you need to give priority this week?
2. Who can help you to execute your plans and strategize effectively?

GRATITUDE *Journey*

Homework:

Carve out one hour per day this week to only work on your business plans. Turn off any distractions and disconnect from people, places, or things that may infringe on your ability to focus. Do everything you can, today, to get it done!

130. I WILL NEVER DO THESE THINGS AGAIN

Transformation begins the moment we're resolute. I've decided that the things that are no good for me, have cost me far more than I thought they would. Consequently, those decisions are too expensive for me and YOU! Our transformation is not only connected to what we do. It is also connected to what we stop doing. "I will never do the things that hurt me again. Transformation starts now." Say that three times and go!

Today I am grateful for:

Introspective/Reflection Questions:

1. If people were to make a documentary about your life, what would be your favorite scene?
2. What would be your least favorite scene? How can you ensure that you don't create an unwanted sequel in your life?

GRATITUDE Journey

Homework:

Gather a few friends together and invite them out to eat. Ask them these questions above, and then finally end with "if you could transform one thing about your life, what would it be?" After everyone answers, create accountability with one another so that transformation can move from imagination to implementation.

131. MY INTEGRITY MUST BE CONSISTENT

I've learned that my integrity must be consistent. People trust people that they can count on. What some call predictable others call consistent. The last thing we should do is allow our questionable character to be the reason other people can't depend on us. The called have to be consistent. It's the only way to be.

Today I am grateful for:

Introspective/Reflection Questions:

1. Do you struggle with consistency? Why or why not?
2. Who is the most consistent person in your life? What do you admire most about them?

GRATITUDE Journey

Homework:

Call the most consistent person in your life and tell them thank you. It's a simple homework assignment, but it will make a world of difference! Once you start speaking to them, don't rush off the phone. See if they need anything, if you can offer them any assistance, and take some time to encourage them today.

132. I WILL INSPIRE OTHERS TO WALK IN INTEGRITY

The greatest evangelism tool we have is our lives, NOT our lips. People prefer to see what we do as opposed to what we say. A life of consistency and integrity speaks volumes. I will inspire others to walk in integrity by my life, NOT my lips.

Today I am grateful for:

Introspective/Reflection Questions:

1. What does "integrity" mean to you?
2. How have you demonstrated integrity in your home, at your job, or in school?

GRATITUDE *Journey*

Homework:

Today, visit Youtube and watch the Ted Talk titled "Building Integrity – Keeping Promises." Take notes and share it with a friend if it speaks to you.

133. MY INTEGRITY WILL PROTECT MY DESTINY

Our future is locked up in our now. Though what will be will be, the amount of time it takes to get there is all in how we handle the present. I've learned that my integrity protects my destiny. Resist the urge to be like the crowd. Follow your heart and stay your course. Your destiny is connected to your discipline.

Today I am grateful for:

Introspective/Reflection Questions:

1. Who is the most protective friend or family member in your life?
2. Do you protect your destiny the way that person you named, protects you?

GRATITUDE Journey

Homework:

Today, think on your life and where you are right now. Write down everything you do, within a 24 hour day, for others, and then write down everything you do, within a 24 hour day, for yourself. Examine, based on your results, if you are truly carving out enough time for your destiny and your dreams.

134. I AM TAKING MY RED CARPET WALK THROUGH SUCCESS

Success isn't just what we see, success is how we see. How do you know when you're winning? That's easy, when you're walking. Take the time to embrace the victory of your now. Today you can decide to embrace the fact that you are not where you were, and you are headed to where you are supposed to be. Walk that red carpet walk of success and don't forget to smile.

Today I am grateful for:

Introspective/Reflection Questions:

1. What is one thing you've accomplished this week? Name it and then celebrate!
2. What is one thing you've accomplished this year? Name it and then celebrate!

GRATITUDE *Journey*

Homework:

Buy two jars from the store. Create a thankfulness jar and a celebration jar. Every time you accomplish something (whether small or big) put it in the celebration jar. Every time you reflect on something you are grateful for, put it in the thankfulness jar. At the end of the year, open up each jar and read what you've written. Celebrate your successes and walk that red carpet into your next season!

135. I WILL DO WHAT IS RIGHT AND GOD WILL PAY

Today, I have decided to do the right thing. When we do what is right, God will pay the balance. Oftentimes we are tempted to handle things OUR way, but when that happens we must also foot the bill. God's way is right, and better. Go with God. That's what I'm going to do.

Today I am grateful for:

Introspective/Reflection Questions:

1. Michelle Obama once said, "when they go low, we go high."
Name a time when you could've gone low, but you decided to go high.
2. What did "going high" teach you about yourself and others?

GRATITUDE *Journey*

Homework:

Come up with a list of 5 ways you will "go high" when different scenarios come your way. For example, "when someone yells at me or speaks to me condescendingly, I will..." or "when someone tries to call me with gossip, I will..." Create 5 scenarios that may happen to you, on any given day, and design a proactive reaction strategy so that you are clear about what you will do before you have to do it.

136. I HAVE THE ABILITY TO CALL THINGS INTO EXISTENCE

The Bible says that we were created in God's image and after His likeness. If the Bible is true, then just as it was in the beginning, so can it be now. Everything that was made, was spoken before it was. I have the ability to call things into existence, just like the beginning. Today I'm using my words.

Today I am grateful for:

Introspective/Reflection Questions:

1. Think about your kids. What do you see in the spirit that you need to speak into existence? Write it down.
2. Think about your spouse or family members. What do you see in the spirit that you need to speak into existence? Write it down.

GRATITUDE Journey

Homework:

Today, listen to Myron Butler's song "Speak," and remember you shall have what you decree. Begin to speak things into the atmosphere with specificity and intentionality.

137. I WILL HAVE WHAT I SAY

You know the expression, "If you don't have anything nice to say, don't say anything at all?" Well, that expression also applies to your life. Choose your words very carefully. If you aren't where you'd like to be, say you haven't arrived YET. If you don't have all the money you need, say you don't have it YET! I will have whatever I say, so what I say matters. Choose your words wisely.

Today I am grateful for:

Introspective/Reflection Questions:

1. What words do you need to delete from your everyday vocabulary? Write those words down below.
2. What words do you need to add to your everyday vocabulary? Write those words down below.

GRATITUDE *Journey*

Homework:

Today reflect on these scriptures and do your best to commit them to memory.

Proverbs 18:21 Death and life are in the power of the tongue: and they that love it shall eat the fruit thereof.
Matthew 16:19 - I will give you the keys of the kingdom of heaven; whatever you bind on earth will be bound in heaven, and whatever you loose on earth will be loosed in heaven."

138. I WILL PAY ATTENTION TO WHAT I AM ATTRACTING

Birds of a feather flock together. Therefore, people judge you by the company you keep. Pay attention to what you're attracting. In this season, you want good vibes only. If they aren't bringing good vibes, then they have to go. Cut the cord.

Today I am grateful for:

Introspective/Reflection Questions:

1. Who are your closest friends? Who do you hang out with the most?
2. Do these people bring you joy, encouragement, peace, and prosperity? Are they adding value to you or taking value away?

GRATITUDE Journey

Homework:

This will be a hard homework assignment, but you need to plan your exit strategy. If someone is sucking the life out of you, and causing you to be less joyful and more anxious, you need to slowly but surely reposition them in your life. Plan this strategy with someone you trust, and someone who will remind you of WHY you needed to do so, as often as you need to hear it.

139. I WILL NOT DESPISE THE CRAWLING STAGE

Before you can run, you must first walk; but before you can walk, you have to crawl. Don't despise the crawling stage. I know you may not be moving as fast as you'd like, but you're still moving. Even if you have to crawl to finish, FINISH.

Today I am grateful for:

Introspective/Reflection Questions:

1. What is happening in your life, in slow motion? In other words, what is something that you wish had happened more quickly, but you see slow results?
2. How can you be gentler with yourself, and more congratulatory about your small progress?

GRATITUDE *Journey*

Homework:

Losing weight is hard, and going to the gym is harder. This week, don't weigh yourself. Don't beat yourself up if you miss a day at the gym. Instead of working out for an hour, work out for 30 minutes. Give yourself permission to graduate slowly. There's no need to rush. You aren't in competition with anyone else, but yourself.

140. I AM READY TO LET IT ALL GO

Wherever you go, the thing(s) you hold onto, go with you as well. It's like traveling through an airport with more bags than you can carry, yet none of them belong to you. Unnecessary baggage weighs us down unnecessarily. Today, I've decided to let it all go and only accept what God has for me. The baggage of my past, others' expectations, and even my personal regret, all of it has to go. Goodbye.

Today I am grateful for:

Introspective/Reflection Questions:

1. Name two emotional/personal weights that you need to let go.
2. Who do you need to say goodbye to you in this season in order to truly walk in full gratitude and undistracted joy?

GRATITUDE Journey

Homework:

Today, watch the sermon titled "Let it Go" by Bishop T.D. Jakes. Take notes and share it on social media with your friends and family. You may end up blessing someone else in the process.

141. MY LIFE MUST BE INTENTIONAL

The Bible says whatever you do, do it with all you have. Every decision, every move, must be intentional. My life must be intentional. I choose to serve others. I choose to give. I choose to be my best self. An intentional life is a life that invites God to bless it. Whatever you do, do it on purpose. Be intentional.

Today I am grateful for:

Introspective/Reflection Questions:

1. How do you define intentionality?
2. What were you very intentinal about today, that brought immediate satisfaction?

GRATITUDE Journey

Homework:

Make a fresh fruit salad as a snack. Instead of rushing to eat it, take a moment and work on your intentional awareness. Pay attention to the size of each item. Utilize all senses and slowly enjoy each delectable bite. The goal is to take 10-15 minutes to eat your fruit as opposed to 3-5 minutes. As you complete this activity, remind yourself to be as intentional about life, as you are about eating this fruit salad.

142. I AM ON THE WISE TRACK TOWARD ACCOMPLISHING MY GOALS

I realized a long time ago that I, myself, don't know much. It's only by the help of God that I am who I am. I choose to use God's wisdom over my intellect every day. God's wisdom transports me to my goal. It's not about me. I am grateful for every goal I have, and every goal I have accomplished. But most of all, I am grateful for a God who guides my steps and tells me which way to go.

Today I am grateful for:

Introspective/Reflection Questions:

1. What is a recent goal that you achieved with God's help?
2. What is a future goal you want to accomplish with God's help?

GRATITUDE *Journey*

Homework:

Today, set this scripture verse to memory:
Proverbs 16:9 - We can make our plans, but the LORD determines our steps.

143. I WILL FOCUS ON LIVING AND NOT DYING

I will focus on living and NOT dying. Many times, when counting up the cost, we focus on what we don't have. The money that we are short. The spouse we wish we had. The school we should've attended. The things and the moments that passed us by. However, the things we do have are staring at us in the face, waiting to be acknowledged. Dead things can't strengthen us. They can't offer words of encouragement. They can't assist us financially. They are dead. As a result, choose to focus on living, not dying. Live a life of fulfillment. Go after your goals and LIVE! Let the dead things stay dead.

Today I am grateful for:

Introspective/Reflection Questions:

1. What has died in your life that you constantly remind yourself of?
2. What can you do to let that go, and focus on the living things?

GRATITUDE *Journey*

Homework:

Journal about this Scripture verse today and identify the areas you need to let go of:

Philippians 3:13 - Brothers and sisters, I do not consider myself yet to have taken hold of it. But one thing I do: Forgetting what is behind and straining toward what is ahead,

144. GOD WILL ALWAYS INTERVENE ON MY BEHALF

One thing for sure, God will always intervene on my behalf. He promises to intercede for us and help us when we need Him. He will never leave and will always offer help. Today, I will remember that and trust him. I will thank him for every divine interception and for every divine interruption. God is so good!

Today I am grateful for:

Introspective/Reflection Questions:

1. Write down one important lesson that a grandparent or an older mentor taught you.
2. How did their intervention, interruption, or sound wisdom help to point you in the right direction?

GRATITUDE *Journey*

Homework:

Today, listen to the song "God Blocked It" by Kurt Carr. Pay attention to the lyrics of each verse, and as you listen, thank God for every situation he blocked, disrupted, or interrupted for your good.

145. I HAVE TO BE MORE FOCUSED THAN EVER

Now is the time to be focused. Now is the time to gain momentum. I will not waste another minute with mindless distractions. I know that something big is on the horizon, so I will focus until I finish. Thankful today for those who have finished before me, as an encouragement to me!

Today I am grateful for:

Introspective/Reflection Questions:

1. Which family member has completed something, in their personal life or in their career, that you admire?
2. Think of someone you have never met personally, but you are inspired by their life, their story, and their focus? What inspires you about them?

GRATITUDE *Journey*

Homework:

Create an acronym that you can remember for the word FOCUS. For example, Follow One Course Until Successful or Finding Original Creative Unique Solutions. Make up one acronym from the word FOCUS and share it with a friend.

146. I WILL BE THE CHANGE I WANT TO SEE IN THE WORLD

Instead of waiting for a "you" to help you, be the you that helps others. Be the change you want to see in the world. When you help others, God will send others to help you. Start with yourself. Be what you need and what you need will show up. Selah.

Today I am grateful for:

Introspective/Reflection Questions:

1. What do you really need to show up in your life over the next 6 months?
2. How can you meet someone else's need, in your family or in your church, over the next 6 months?

GRATITUDE Journey

Homework:

Be a blessing to someone, in a significant way, over the next six months. Since we reap what we sow, expect a harvest to come in your direction as well.

147. MY INTEGRITY WILL ALWAYS GO BEFORE ME

My integrity will always go before me. My name will be in rooms long before I ever get there. My most valuable possession isn't my bank account, my safe, my vault, home, or garage. The most valuable possession I have is my name. Therefore, I will walk wisely. I will listen closely. I will always lead with integrity because God is counting on me to walk justly.

Today I am grateful for:

Introspective/Reflection Questions:

1. What does it mean to "walk wisely" in this season of your life?
2. When was the last time you made an unwise decision, and saw the impact it had on those you loved?

GRATITUDE *Journey*

Homework:

Your health is more important than you know. We are not just what we eat, we are also what we drink. Today, drink more water than you ever have before. Allow your body to be cleansed by the purity of water, and challenge yourself to increase your water intake daily.

148. I WILL WELCOME JESUS INTO MY LIFE

Jesus never overstays his welcome. Jesus doesn't force himself on anyone. When we invite Him into the secret spaces of our hearts, He does what He does best. Today, make the decision to welcome Him. He won't knock down the door of your heart, instead, he'll wait until you let him in. Once He's there, you'll never want Him to leave. Try Him. Thank Him. Love him.

Today I am grateful for:

Introspective/Reflection Questions:

1. When did you give your life to Christ and accept him as Lord?
2. How do you know that God is real in your life? How can you encourage someone else to know him today?

GRATITUDE Journey

Homework:

Today, reflect on your journey. Whether you have a vibrant relationship with God or a rocky one, sit for a moment and think about all you have endured, overcome, and triumphed over. Be still and reflect. Then share your testimony/experience with someone you don't know.

149. AND IT CAME TO PASS

One day you're going to get what you prayed for. You've been sowing in tears. You've been fasting and believing. I believe that soon you're going to tell the story of what you needed, what only God could do, and at the end of that story, gently, quietly, and softly you're going to say...and it came to pass. Just hold on. Your time is now.

Today I am grateful for:

Introspective/Reflection Questions:

1. What do you want God to bring to pass for a loved one today?
2. What do you need God to bring to pass for you?

GRATITUDE *Journey*

Homework:

Find three Scriptures in the Bible that contain the words "and it came to pass" within them. Study them and share them. Use them as inspirational tools to motivate you to believe that God can do it for you, and your loved ones, too!

150. I AM headed to my prayer room

I'm convinced that nothing happens by chance. Everything we need is birthed through time with God. The safest place you can be is in prayer. Seek shelter. I'm headed to my prayer room. I'm prepared to tell God thank you—thank you for this journey, thank you for the joys; thank you for the sorrows—thank you for it all! All of it taught me a lesson I needed to learn in life, and for that, I will forever express gratitude.

Today I am grateful for:

Introspective/Reflection Questions:

1. What is the highest moment or memory you've experienced over this Gratitude Journey? How did God reveal himself in that?
2. What is the lowest moment or memory you've experienced over this Gratitude Journey? How did God reveal himself in that?

Homework:

Write one final thank you letter to every person who matters to you. The letter can be long or short. You can record a video, or a voice note. But long after you take your last breath, let it be said that your "thank you" lived beyond you. Remember: gratitude is a gift we give ourselves. And once we fully embody it, it has the power to change the world!

A WOMAN OF GRACE, POISE & EXCELLENCE

Ylawnda Peebles is the exultant wife of 27 years to her best friend, Senior Pastor, Joel R. Peebles, Sr., and she is Co-Pastor of the City of Praise Family Ministries in Landover, Maryland. Together, they are blessed to have four amazing and brilliant children – Joel, Jr., Janay, Jordan and Jeremiah. Ylawnda is a graduate of Bowie State University, where she graduated with high honors earning the Magna Cum Laude Award, she has her Master's Degree in Divinity from Wilbur Henry Waters School of Divinity, a Doctorate of Divinity from Rivers Bible Institute and a Doctorate in Humane Letters from Breakthrough Bible College.

In 2003 she founded Heart to Heart Literacy Program. This non-profit charitable organization was designed to inspire literacy in school aged children. She also wrote and published a children's book entitled, "God Loves Me Just the Way I Am", which is in its 3rd printing. She assists hundreds of women on their journey to health and wholeness through her efforts with her Transformation Squad, Kingdom Queen Organization, and the YP Rise Up Gratitude Journey, a live show on Facebook. Ylawnda co-hosts many ministry affairs such as the "Marry Me Again Experience" Marriage Events, "Touching the Hearts of People" telecast aired on the Impact Network, the Word of the Day aired on both Praise 104.1 and 105.1 WAVA stations in the Washington, DC Metropolitan Area.

Ylawnda was humbled and honored to receive the Coretta Scott King Award from the Prince George's Chapter of the Southern Christian Leadership Conference, the Catalyst of the Year Award from the Prince George's Chapter of Jack & Jill, Top Walk Team/Top Walker Fundraiser from NAMI Maryland, and Top Ten First Ladies from Praise 104.1.

Ylawnda is a member of the Alpha Kappa Alpha Sorority, Incorporated, and is faithfully committed to service for all mankind. She was grateful to receive, "New Soror of the Year in 2018.

"An empty life only focuses on personal achievement. True happiness is trusting in God, loving your family and making a substantial impact on one's community."

– Ylawnda Peebles

Made in the USA
Middletown, DE
01 November 2020

Hold On
Pain Ends

All of us have a story. Some of those stories come with scars; and let's face it: scars are painful. But the good news is, the pain ends. In this beautiful devotional journal, Ylawnda Peebles teaches us the beauty of an often overlooked gift: the gift of GRATITUDE. This book is for those who want more than modification; this book is for those who need transformation. Hold On Pain Ends is a journey of hope that was written to help women find holistic health: spiritually, physically, and emotionally. By the end of these 150 glorious days, you will tap into a freedom that brings complete joy, in every area of your life!

Ylawnda Peebles

ISBN 978-1-942705-   -8
$2
52 99>

YP GRATITUDE
Journey

The Art of
Boot & Shoemaking

A Practical Handbook

Including

Measurement, Last-Fitting, Cutting-Out, Closing, and Making

With a Description of the Most Approved Machinery Employed

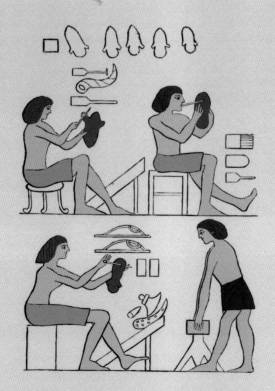

JOHN BEDFORD LENO